THE END OF THE KEYNESIAN ERA

THE END OF THE KEYNESIAN ERA

KEYNESIAN ERA

Essays on the disintegration of the Keynesian political economy

Edited by
Robert Skidelsky

Contributors:
Robert Skidelsky, John Vaizey, Marcello de Cecco, Peter Lilley, Samuel Brittan, Aubrey Jones, Robert Lekachman, Stuart Holland, J. T. Winkler, Harry G. Johnson, David P. Calleo and Geoffrey Barraclough

HOLMES & MEIER PUBLISHERS, INC.
IMPORT DIVISION
IUB Building
30 Irving Place, New York, N.Y. 10003

First edition 1977
Reprinted 1978

Published by
THE MACMILLAN PRESS LTD
London and Basingstoke
Associated companies in Delhi Dublin
Hong Kong Johannesburg Lagos Melbourne
New York Singapore Tokyo

Printed in Great Britain by
BILLING & SONS LTD
Worcester, Guildford and London

HB99.7
E53
1977

British Library Cataloguing in Publication Data

The end of the Keynesian era
  1.   Economic history — 20th century — Addresses,
essays, lectures
  I.   Skidelsky, Robert
  330.9'04   HC54

ISBN 0–333–21298–3   Hardcover
ISBN 0–333–21306–8   Pbk

Contents

Preface

These essays appeared in the *Spectator* between May 1976 and January 1977, most of them in shortened form. I should like to thank Mrs Jenny Naipaul of the *Spectator* for her helpfulness and efficiency, which greatly eased the task of transforming that series into this book.

R. S.

Introduction

I have tried to assemble a collection of essays whose focus is on the malfunctioning of our present system of political economy. The use of the phrase 'political economy' is deliberate and, in my view, helpful to understanding. Once government started to assume substantial responsibility for economic affairs, the old separation between politics and economics broke down. In the nineteenth century it was possible and usual to believe that economic life would be affected to a decreasing extent by political 'interference'. This was based on two, complementary, assumptions. The first was that there existed economic laws which, if followed, would maximise everyone's advantage. The second was that certain political, institutional, and psychological conditions could be taken for granted, notably the hegemony of what Keynes was to call the 'educated bourgeoisie', who would understand these economic laws, and the environment necessary for their successful application. The twentieth century has invalidated both these assumptions. Unregulated economic systems proved liable to crippling fluctuations. And, with the growth of democracy, political tolerance for these fluctuations markedly declined. As a result, government took responsibility for stabilising economic activity at a high-enough level of output to maintain something like full employment. This meant, inevitably, that a large area of economic action now depended on political, not market, processes. If political process is more broadly defined, to include bargaining between organised producer groups over such matters as wages and prices, it is apparent how large a segment of contemporary economic life has become 'politicised'. This means that economic action can be less and less explained by theories dealing with the behaviour of individuals acting in the marketplace; that economic problems, such as inflation, have their roots in political, not economic, logic. It used to be thus in the mercantilist era; and our own has aptly been called 'neo-mercantilist' for this reason.

Strangely, at the point in time when real life has been forcing politics and economics together, the two disciplines are becoming more and more separated through the further progress of the intellectual division of labour. Basic economic principles as expounded by, say, John Stuart Mill in the middle of the nineteenth century were still accessible to the educated man. Today economics is understood only by the specialist. In Mill's time, the principles of government were also thought to be clearly established and readily comprehensible. Today unique understanding of them is claimed by political scientists. The language of the two disciplines has thus moved apart even as their content has come together. It may be that specialisation has proceeded to the point where it is becoming counterproductive for the understanding of real-life situations. It is a tribute to the contributors to this volume that it would be difficult to glean from their essays exactly where their academic specialisation lies. They have accepted the challenge to 'think big' about big issues.

The use of the adjective 'Keynesian' to describe our present system of political economy is also deliberate. It is open to three objections.

The first runs as follows. Government intervention in twentieth century economic life has been growing for many different reasons – for humanitarian or socialist reasons, for reasons of war, for reasons of changing economic structure, because of the growth of democracy, and so on. The result is often known as the 'mixed economy'. Why attach the label Keynesian to it? The reason is that Keynes, more than anyone else, determined what the mixture should be. Keynes alone provided an intellectually coherent justification for a certain type of government intervention, one which would save, not destroy, both capitalism and liberal democracy (see Chapter 5 of this book). We have put his theory into operation and lived by it for the last thirty years. Before Keynes, most 'advanced' thinkers believed that some system of authoritarian planning, usually modelled on Russia, was the only answer to the economic problem. Keynes provided an alternative model, an alternative theory of how the economy works, and fails to

work, with its in-built policy prescriptions. For the intelligentsia, inside and outside the economic profession, it was essential to have such a theory. Mere inflationism would never have
been accepted as a reputable alternative to centralised planning. The change in intellectual atmosphere from the 1930s to
the 1950s and 1960s is striking. This was largely the work of
Keynes.

A second objection to calling our political economy Keynesian comes from the Marxists. To call it Keynesian, they say,
is to obscure its connection with the old capitalism, its in-
justices, contradictions, and instability. At best Keynes post-
poned the final crisis, at the cost of intensifying its contradictions. Despite the force of this, the label Keynesian is
analytically useful. It draws attention to a crucial development which Marxists tend to deny: the decline in the political
power of private capital. This power has steadily receded in
face of the growth of working-class organisation and the state.
It was this change in the balance of social power that enabled
Keynesian ideas to triumph in the first place. No doubt big
business needed Keynes too, and appropriated Keynesian
spending policies for its own advantage. But need for state
economic support is a sign of weakness, not strength; and full
employment was a labour, not business, demand, commitment to which has, in turn, strengthened labour's bargaining
power. Of course, concentrated private capital is still im-
mensely strong. But it no longer dominates the stage as it did
fifty or sixty years ago; and in Britain and Italy it has been
substantially, perhaps fatally, weakened. The modern
problem of inflation arises, in part, precisely because government and workers are able to appropriate increasing shares of
an insufficiently growing national product. Today's 'central
economic issue' is defined by Robert Lekachman (Chapter 8)
as 'reconciliation within the framework of political democracy
and private ownership . . . . of group claims for more of the
national product than can be made available'. This was *not* the
problem when capitalism ruled the roost, and the adjective
Keynesian draws attention to the difference, and its nature.

A third objection to the use of the adjective Keynesian takes
the form of denying that Keynesian ideas were in fact that central to the libertarian prosperity of the post-war world. In contrast to the conventional view that 'the widespread absorption

of the Keynesian message has in large measure been responsible for the remarkable degree of economic stability in the Western world' since the war (William J. Barber, *A History of Economic Thought* (1967), p. 257), David P. Calleo (Chapter 12) reminds us that 'the "Age of Keynes" has also been, after all, the *Pax Americana*', and that 'Keynesian national economic policies, whatever their own tendencies, have had to be conducted within an international order which has, itself, certain definite tendencies which it transmits to national systems'. The argument is that America's hegemony freed it from the payments discipline which America was able to impose on other powers. America was able to run a deficit on its balance of payments for the better part of three decades. It was this deficit, rather than the combined results of domestic Keynesian management, which produced both world prosperity and inflation. The argument deserves serious attention. Yet even if we give the prolonged American deficits pride of place in sustaining post-war prosperity, can they be separated from the influence of Keynes? It was Keynes, after all, who legitimised deficits of all kinds, by explaining the mechanisms whereby injections in spending power would promote employment and prosperity. In a sense, America can be regarded as having played a Keynesian role on a (free) world scale. At any rate, it is highly doubtful whether either the Americans themselves or the Europeans would have accepted prolonged American deficits without the understanding of their economic function which Keynes provided. And the world inflation to which they helped give rise is part of the general problem of the Keynesian political economy.

The major assumption of most, if not all, of the contributors to this volume is that our contemporary system of political economy is unstable. What will follow? Although three of the contributors (Peter Lilley, Samuel Brittan and Harry G. Johnson) believe that government intervention has already gone too far, the majority appear to accept that the future will (and perhaps should) bring more government control over economic life than Keynes would have considered desirable (though both Lekachman and Geoffrey Barraclough find such further extensions implicit in Keynes himself). Developments and events are forcing the state to do more things in the economy than Keynes wanted and, as J. T. Winkler says in

Chapter 10, 'there is a different logic to how these should be done'. Planning of production and incomes will become permanent; there will be new policies to reduce inequality; public ownership will probably be extended.

A number of questions arise. Are such views to be seen as statements about what will happen or statements about what should happen? One point is worth emphasising. Statements implying a reduction of the government's economic role are almost invariably of the 'should' variety; while those implying an increase in the government's economic role almost invariably take the form of predictions based on current trends. It may be that those who say that such-and-such should happen too often ignore what is actually happening; while those who argue from the trend too often ignore the power of ideas and events to alter trends.

A second problem concerns the name we should give to the political economy beyond Keynes. For those in the Marxist tradition, capitalism will give way to socialism. Such developments as planning, wage–price controls, and so on, can be interpreted as extensions of socialism, particularly if buttressed by further public ownership and the growth of industrial democracy as advocated by Stuart Holland (Chapter 9). Winkler, on the other hand, argues that they are best understood as 'the coming corporatism', a system of state control over a predominantly privately-owned economy: a model obviously derived from fascism.

A third problem, related to the last, has to do with the political implications of such extensions of state activity. Can democracy survive them? The habit of assigning politically bland names to the state's growth (for instance, planning), obscures its political consequences. Commenting on an influential recent argument in favour of more equality. Robert Nisbet remarks: 'The mind boggles at the thought of the political apparatus necessary to give expression to and enforce such a principle. ... Rawls [in *The Theory of Justice* (1972)] seems never to have heard of political bureaucracy' (*The Twilight of Authority* (1975), p. 216).

Finally, whatever may be the tendencies, ideas or events promoting new developments in our system of political economy, they are not identical in every country. Keynes has been a dominating influence on post-war public policy in Britain, and to a lesser extent, the United States (see Herbert Stein's classic *The Fiscal Revolution in America* (1969)). Harry G. Johnson suggests (in Chapter 11) that Keynesian ideas have been influential, though largely unsuccessful, in the developing countries. But it would be interesting to know just how much influence Keynes has had on the way economics is taught and applied in such countries as Germany, France, Japan and Italy. Perhaps the worldwide sweep of the Keynesian political economy has had more to do with the post-war Anglo-American hegemony than with the existence of well-established domestic 'Keynesian' traditions. In any event, such unity as Keynesian ideas may have given to the post-war economic system is unlikely to survive its present travails. Many flowers will bloom in the years ahead, including, no doubt, some exotic ones.

Robert Skidelsky

Notes on the Contributors

Robert Skidelsky. Historian. Head of the Department of History and Philosophy, Polytechnic of North London. Author of *Politicians and the Slump* and *Oswald Mosley;* at present writing a life of Keynes.

Lord Vaizey. Economist. Sometime Fellow of St Catharine's College, Cambridge, and Fellow and Tutor of Worcester College, Oxford. Professor of Economics at Brunel University. Author of *Social Democracy*, etc.

Marcello de Cecco. Economist. Professor of Monetary Economics, University of Siena. Author of *Money and Empire*.

Peter Lilley. Economic consultant and investment analyst. Former chairman of the Bow Group. Author of *Do you Sincerely Want to Win?*, *Controlling Inflation,* and (with Samuel Brittan) *The Delusion of Incomes Policy.*

Samuel Brittan. Economics commentator of the *Financial Times*. Visiting Fellow, Nuffield College, Oxford. Author of numerous books and essays, including *Left or Right: The Bogus Dilemma, Capitalism and the Permissive Society, Second Thoughts on Full Employment Policy.*

Rt. Hon. Aubrey Jones. Conservative politician. Minister of Fuel and Power 1955–7; Minister of Supply 1957–9. Chairman, National Board for Prices and Incomes, 1965–70. Author of *Industrial Order* and *The New Inflation: The Politics of Prices and Incomes.*

Robert Lekachman. Economist. Professor of Economics at

Herbert H. Lehman College, New York. Author of *A History of Economic Ideas, The Age of Keynes,* etc.

Stuart Holland. Historian and economist. Lecturer in European Studies, Sussex University. Cabinet Office 1966–7; Prime Minister's Political Office 1967–8. Member of various sub-committees of the Labour Party's National Executive Committee since 1971. Author of *The Socialist Challenge, The Regional Problem,* etc.; editor of *The State as Entrepreneur.*

J. T. Winkler. Sociologist. Lecturer at Cranfield Institute of Technology. Author of *The Coming Corporatism* (to be published shortly).

Harry G. Johnson. Economist. Until his death in May 1977, Charles F. Grey Distinguished Service Professor of Economics at the University of Chicago, and Professor of Economics at the Graduate Institute of International Studies, Geneva. Author of *International Trade and Economic Growth, Economic Policies Toward the Less Developed Countries, Essays in Monetary Economics,* etc.

David P. Calleo. Political theorist. Professor of European Studies at the Johns Hopkins School of Advanced International Studies. Author of *Europe's Future, Britain's Future, The Atlantic Fantasy* (with Benjamin Rowland), *America and the World Political Economy,* etc.

Geoffrey Barraclough. Historian. Chichele Professor of Modern History, University of Oxford, and Fellow of All Souls College, 1970–3. His many books include *Mediaeval Germany, The Mediaeval Empire, The Mediaeval Papacy,* and *An Introduction to Contemporary History.*

1 The Revolt against the Victorians

ROBERT SKIDELSKY

'We cannot base our hopes for the future upon a resumption of the cheap and easy living standards of the past. . . . We shall have to level down a bit.' So ran a characteristic prediction of 1949. If any one person can be credited with falsifying it, it is John Maynard Keynes. Born in 1883 and dying in 1946, he had, seemingly, bequeathed to politicians the economic equivalent of the Philosopher's Stone – the ability to turn slumps into booms, and so to create general and permanent abundance for the first time in history. Today we are starting to suspect that we have been cheated once again. But Keynes's achievement was more solid than that of the old alchemist, and his name deserves to be given to an era which created at any rate the 'possibility of civilisation' for the peoples of the West.

How did Keynes come to invent Keynesian economics? An exhaustive answer would have to take into account his quality of mind, his personal motivation, the distinctive tradition of Cambridge economics, the challenge of the Depression, and so on. What I should like to do here is to trace his economic originality back to a changed attitude to life dating from his days in Cambridge and London in the 1900s. This new attitude was not confined to Keynes. It was shared also by other Cambridge and London founders of what came to be the Bloomsbury Group. At its centre was an overwhelming sense that life was to be lived for the present, not for the past or the future. As such it involved jettisoning many of the Puritan values dear to the Victorians, including those of Keynes's own family and the older Cambridge generation. I believe it was this vision which drove him to stand out, in his chosen field of economics, against the Victorian restoration attempted in the inter-war years. At the same time, the impatient urge to clear

1

the ground for intelligent and beautiful living led him gravely to underestimate the difficulties of breaking through to permanent prosperity, especially for a country in Britain's situation. In that sense he can be criticised for generalising from the particularly favoured situation of his own milieu in Edwardian Cambridge.

The attempt to ground the Keynesian Revolution in a new consciousness may, but should not, shock the professional economist. Every economic system depends on an appropriate psychic disposition or 'ethic'. The most famous association of this kind is between Protestantism and capitalism. Max Weber argued that the intense anxiety created by the Calvinist doctrine of predestination produced a 'worldly ascetic' ethic favourable to capitalism. In particular, the notion of a goal-directed life, in which a plan of projects to be achieved is methodically geared to limited resources of time and energy, was essential for the development of capitalist rationality. It is hardly surprising, then, that the shift in economic priorities implied by the Keynesian revolution should have had its basis in a changed 'ethic'. The link between the two lies in the radical demotion of 'saving' or 'abstinence'. For, as Keynes well recognised, the economic doctrine of saving embodied a principle of living adopted by Victorian society as a whole. The assault on saving which runs right through Keynes's economic writings can, in my view, be traced directly to his changed personal ethic. The social and political acceptance of the Keynesian Revolution in economics can, in turn, be traced, in part, to a changed social consciousness whose material base was provided by the beginning of a mass consumption economy in the late nineteenth century.

The Victorian background was very much Keynes's own. His mother, Florence Ada Brown, was descended from a bewildering succession of Puritan divines. One of them, the Reverend Everard Ford, an Independent Congregational clergyman, sublimated his forbidden passion for music into vigorous denunciations of human evil. Maynard Keynes's maternal grandfather, the Reverend John Brown, author of a best-selling life of Bunyan, read Gladstone's speeches as Chancellor of the Exchequer round the family hearth. Keynes's father, John Neville Keynes, an economics don of

Pembroke College, Cambridge, is remembered by Bertrand Russell as an 'earnest non-conformist who put morality first and logic second'. At all times, according to Keynes's mother, 'a high standard of moral and intellectual effort' was demanded from members of her family. Keynes's childhood and schooldays, though, seem to have been reasonably happy; and a belief in intellectual excellence, and its hereditary character, was the one aspect of his family's 'ethic' which he adopted without question.

Keynes was born not just into a family but into a particular Victorian culture. The psychology of the 'intellectual aristocracy' which moulded the character of nineteenth-century Cambridge (and much of Britain) has been discussed in a suggestive essay by Lord Annan. Annan describes the nature and spreading influence of a handful of wealthy, late eighteenth-century, Evangelical families (the Clapham Sect) to which were joined a cluster of Quaker and Unitarian families. They were first brought together by the anti-slavery agitation; they continued to work together in liberal and philanthropic causes; finally they intermarried simply because their children never met anyone else, forming an ever-widening cousinhood of patronage and influence. They exhibited all the familiar Puritan features. Life was a constant battle against sin disguised as pleasure. Of Sir James Stephen, Leslie Stephen's father, it was said that he 'once smoked a cigar and found it so delicious he never smoked again'. Improvement was the overriding aim – their own and the world's. Overwhelmingly conscious of time, they had little time to spare for art and beauty. Recreation was a preparation for further effort.

The opinions, attitudes, and concerns of this intellectual cousinhood formed part of the mental and physical atmosphere in which Keynes grew up. The traumatic experience of the previous generation had been the loss of religious faith. At Cambridge, Henry Sidgwick and Leslie Stephen had wrestled interminably with their 'doubts' before reaching a characteristic Victorian compromise: 'I know I believe in nothing . . . but I do not the less believe in morality', wrote Leslie Stephen. But the Puritan moral code, resting, as Quentin Bell has noted, on 'unstable psychological elements', could not long survive the loss of its religious supports and the spread of leisured affluence. Out of this cultural tradition grew both Bloomsbury's aesthetic ideal and the secular morality of upper-class socialism. The clash between the two, between psychological and social radicalism, is part of the history of twentieth-century English progressivism.

In the formation of Keynes's personal 'ethic', two names stand out: G. E. Moore and Lytton Strachey. He met them in his first term at King's College, Cambridge. They were leading lights in the Apostles, an élite discussion society to which Strachey got Keynes elected in his second term (February 1903). Of Moore's impact on Keynes there can be no real doubt. Thirty-five years later Keynes referred to the publication of Moore's *Principia Ethica* as 'the beginning of a new renaissance, the opening of a new heaven on earth', adding that 'its effect on us ... dominated, and perhaps still dominates everything else'. This was said just after the publication of Keynes's own *General Theory*.

Moore provided his young Cambridge friends with both a method and a message. He mounted a devastating assault on the main intellectual supports of Victorian morality. Moore said that 'good' cannot be defined. Attempts to define it in terms of natural qualities he called the 'naturalistic fallacy'. He then showed that traditional morality, by identifying good with pleasant or progressive or 'willed by God', rested on the naturalistic fallacy. Of this part of the book, Strachey wrote exuberantly: 'And the wreckage! That indiscriminate heap of shattered rubbish among which one spies the utterly mangled remains of Aristotle, Jesus, Mr. Bradley, Kant, Herbert Spencer and McTaggart. . . . Poor Mill has simply gone. . . .' Having demolished the intellectual basis of traditional morality, Moore suggested that the highest goods, those 'good in themselves', are 'certain states of consciousness, which may be roughly described as the pleasures of human intercourse, and the enjoyment of beautiful objects'.

As has often been pointed out, this is a selective interpretation of Moore. Unlike Leonard Woolf, Keynes ignored the chapter dealing with conduct, in which Moore adopted the classical utilitarian standard that an action must be judged by its consequences. Here I think the influence of Strachey was important. What Moore did for Strachey was to justify an aesthetic ideal. As Michael Holroyd points out, Strachey 'turned his back on ethics in relation to conduct'. Keynes followed him. He was fascinated and influenced by the older man. He made the aesthetic ideal his own, becoming, in his own words, an 'immoralist'.

What this entailed for one's attitude to life is described by Keynes himself in 'My Early Beliefs', a talk he gave in 1938. First, and foremost, it shifted the emphasis of life from the public to the private sphere. 'It furnishes', Keynes said, 'a justification of experience wholly independent of outside events.' Economics as a mere science of 'means' ranked much below those things which Moore called 'good in themselves'. Duty and obligation, public virtues, were similarly devalued. Secondly, and closely related to this, it shifted emphasis from the future to the present. This was the radical consequence of making the greatest goods states of mind – which are, by definition, experienced always and only in the present. Moore set on a pedestal the very things the Puritan ethic had most devalued – personal relations and enjoyment of beauty. The object of the Puritan system of self-discipline was to destroy the spontaneous joy of living so as to free time and energy for the serious business of piling up money and achievements for the greater glory of God and the security of one's immortal soul. By contrast, Moore's philosophy emphasised the absolute value of living in the present. His 'highest states of mind', says Keynes, 'are largely unattached to "before" or "after" '. Goethe's famous lines sum up the aesthetic credo: 'Then to the passing moment I would say, Thou art so beautiful, wilt thou not stay?' Keynes could not match the poetry of this in his equally famous remark: 'In the long run we are all dead'; but its spirit is the same – which is that we need a system of economics to enable us to enjoy life now, not in the future when we shall be dead. In shifting the basis of economic speculation from the long run to the short run he was being true to Moore's credo.

In both method and message, Moore's book 'fitted' its time and place. Its starting point was the breakdown of a religious or metaphysical view of the world; but experiments in styles of living could still be projected against a secure social background and mounting prosperity. Beauty could briefly take the place of Morality in the slow dissolution of Absolute Values. And after Beauty? Moore's was emphatically not a hedonist philosophy. But it opened the way to hedonism. 'Everyone would be a hedonist if he could', Keynes wrote in 1905. It gradually became easier. 'As time wore on towards the nineteen-tens, I fancy we weakened a bit about pleasure', he recalled in 1938. Pleasure, wrote Leonard Woolf, came to be accepted as 'a very considerable good in itself'. The psychological foundations had been laid for a fully-fledged anti-Puritan economics.

'Our prime objects in life were love, the creation and enjoyment of aesthetic experience and the pursuit of knowledge. Of these love came a long way first.' Thus Keynes recalled his pre-war Cambridge and London days. How far does the evidence bear this out?

As far as love goes, one of the chief difficulties is to decide how much was talk and how much was action. Keynes and his friends were all very inhibited young men and one should not take their language of love too literally, especially at first. Whether they were sexual or platonic, personal relations were clearly supremely important for Keynes at this and at all periods of his life, though the relentless application of Moore's 'method' to their analysis produces a comic, and sometimes grotesque, impression on the outsider (it had that effect on D. H. Lawrence). Keynes himself was equally susceptible to beauty and intelligence. The trouble was, he complained to Strachey, the two were so rarely combined. Strachey himself was brilliant but hideous. A. L. Hobhouse, Keynes's first Cambridge love, was beautiful but not bright. The painter Duncan Grant, whose great friendship with Keynes started in 1908, combined beauty and talent in a way which must have been deeply satisfying to Keynes's state of mind.

That Keynes's milieu and tastes at this time were predominantly homosexual is now fairly widely known. Strachey certainly construed Moore's teaching as furnishing a justification for homosexuality. Homosexuality is the quintessentially useless passion, in the sense that it has no purpose outside itself (unlike heterosexuality, whose biological purpose is procreation). As such it was the most radical of the assaults on the Victorian principle of living, particularly in its weakening of the motive for saving or accumulation. To ignore the possible influence of its 'childless perspective' on Keynes's attitude to life, and thus on his life's work, would be biographical philistinism.

For Keynes, love and beauty were closely connected. He displayed a quite un-Puritan delight in the human body, photographing the nude sculptures he and Duncan Grant discovered in Greece in 1910. At the same time, he was highly conscious of beauty for its own sake, of the sight, touch and sound of things, whether Impressionist paintings or Diaghilev ballets; the shape of people's hands, antiquarian books, or the valleys of Aragon to which he dreamt of retiring with Duncan Grant. To some Keynes seemed too cautious, too calculating, ever to be a true acolyte of the cult of beauty. He seems to have felt this to be a defect in himself, which he tried to overcome, devoting much of his life to the acquisition and appreciation of beautiful objects in conscious pursuit of Moore's ideal.

Finally, there is his attitude to work, the touchstone of the Puritan ethic. Without doubt he derived enormous pleasure from mental activity. Working at the statistics of verification had sent him into a state of tremendous excitement, he reported to Grant in 1908. The theory of probability also claimed his passionate, if intermittent, interest. Indeed, the characteristic of Keynes's work patterns is precisely that they were intermittent. He worked with intense concentration on things which interested him – the reverse of the Puritan notion of work as a 'calling'. His incredible quickness of mind enabled him to make brilliant intellectual contributions, while reserving the major part of his interest and energy for his friends and the *avant-garde* culture of London.

Equally striking in the period before 1914 was his lack of interest in public affairs at one of the most turbulent moments in British history. His brief spell at the India Office (1906–8) gave him a contempt for public life – 'it is simply government by dotardry' – and he fled back to a fellowship at King's with relief. 'You haven't I suppose ever mixed with politicians at close quarters', he wrote Duncan Grant in 1911. 'They're awful . . . their stupidity is inhuman. . . .' He was also completely uninvolved in the politics of the Left. The Fabians occasionally impinged on his life because Rupert Brooke was interested in them. He was drawn into helping the Suffragettes on one occasion, on behalf of Strachey's sisters. Industrial disputes meant interruptions of train services between Cambridge and London. Keynes's lack of involvement in public affairs should not be overdrawn – he was president of the Cambridge Union and served on the Royal Commission on Indian Finance and Currency – but in general one is struck by his indifference to public life at one of its most momentous periods.

In summary, I am not claiming that Keynesian economics can be 'reduced to' Keynes's new 'ethic' worked out in pre-1914 Cambridge and London. At the same time, this new attitude to life does explain the violence of his hostility to the Victorian restoration attempted in the 1920s – a restoration affecting both economic policy (return to gold) and the arts (increased censorship). It was his commitment to the present which underlay his hostility to saving and thus helped him identify 'over-saving' as the cause of the Depression.

His rejection of Puritanism also helps explain his political attitudes, which in turn affected his interpretation of the economic problem. The Webbs, Shaw, and socialists in general, attributed economic distress to a social institution, capitalism. Keynes identified it with a social psychology, Puritanism. The basis of this difference is reasonably clear. The Webbs and Shaw were moralists in the central Victorian tradition, dedicated to the Victorian struggle for improvement, and to the Puritan virtues traditionally associated with it. Keynes was an 'immoralist', impatient that people should enjoy life in the here and now. Beatrice Webb saw the conflict clearly enough. 'Why don't you', she wrote to the Bloomsbury novelist E. M. Forster, 'write another great novel giving the essence of the current conflict between those who aim at exquisite relationships between the closed circle of the "elect" and those who aim for the hygienic and scientific improvement of the whole of the race?' What appalled Keynes about this programme was the further postponement of civilisation which it implied. To the Webbs travelling was more important than arriving. The Age of Plenty, he would have replied, had already dawned. The fruits of past abstinence could now be enjoyed, provided human affairs were run with a minimal intelligence. The Depression itself was a 'transient muddle', not the mortal sickness of capitalism.

Thus his own personal ideal directly affected his economic work. The First World War, he recognised, had generalised the decay of the Puritan ethic. It had, he wrote, 'disclosed the possibility of consumption to all and the vanity of abstinence

to many'. There could be no going back. The task of the
Apostles in the wider world was to ensure that the Age of
Plenty be beautiful, not vulgar. In the depth of the Depression
he wrote, 'If I had the power today I should surely set out to
endow our capital cities with all the appurtenances of art and
civilisation on the highest standards of which the citizens of
each were individually capable, convinced that what I could
create, I could afford. . . . For with what we have spent on the
dole in England since the war we could have made our cities
the greatest works of man in the world.'

2 Keynes and Cambridge

John Vaizey

For seventy years or so, from 1880 to 1950, Cambridge economics dominated the British intellectual scene. After 1930 the London School of Economics began its career as the British embassy of the Austrian–American school of extreme *laissez-faire*, and Manchester provided a steady muttering of 'industry, competition, cotton'. But the ideas and excitement came from St John's, Trinity and King's. The reason for this was simple. Alfred Marshall imposed himself; and his pupils, of whom J. M. Keynes was one of the youngest, kept up his reputation for nearly thirty years after his death. Marshall was the greatest English economist. Without him, Keynes would have had a very different career and reputation.

Born in 1844, son of a Bank of England clerk, Marshall read mathematics at Cambridge. He became a Fellow of St John's, became the first Principal of what was to become Bristol University, a Fellow of Balliol teaching Indian civil servants, and then came back to Cambridge as Professor of Political Economy. Marshall was a valetudinarian, almost always ailing, but he had the remorseless invalid's quality of persistence. He married Mary Paley, a brilliant girl from Newnham. Childless, she was pushed into the service of his genius. Working in quarter-of-an-hour spurts, he ploughed through economics, unwilling to publish, delaying and delaying, but surrounding himself with brilliant pupils whom he sent into the world to do good. Marshall had the moral fervour of the late Victorian unbelievers. He also had their omniscience. He toured factories, visited trade unions, and could tell to the nearest farthing what people earned. Nobody has ever known more about the British economy; nobody has ever read wider and deeper in the literature of the social sciences. His influence was immense.

First of all, he believed in moral improvement through good works. His pupils were not to sit on their bottoms theorising; he found mathematics dizzily exciting and, like chess, put it behind him. The poor were always with him and their poverty cried out for relief. His powerful mind was perfectly capable of drawing up abstract schemes, but his emphasis was put continually on the hard, recalcitrant stuff of reality. This led him to two other characteristics of his thought – time, and partial equilibrium analysis.

The abstract systems, like those of Menger and Walras, in Austria and Lausanne, made timeless general equilibrium the basis of their work. Everything depended upon everything else simultaneously, so their economics took the form of an infinitely extensible system of simultaneous equations. This had two benefits – no evidence was relevant to whether the system was true or not, since it was self-containedly logical, and it also carried the political message that any interference by government with one bit altered, for the worse, all the rest. In these systems prices, including wages, were infinitely flexible and the market was always cleared. Marshall, on the other hand, believed that circumstances alter cases and in particular that time was the clue to the development of an economy. As the economy moved on through time, the very short run (in which very little could change) was differentiated from the normal period, and from the long run, in which everything (population, ideas, the stock of capital) could be changed. This idea of three sorts of period is fundamental to Cambridge economics; no Cambridge economist can think in any other terms, and it most sharply differentiates Cambridge from the market-clearing simultaneity of the Austrian–LSE school, which elevates relative prices to an absolutely dominant role. Marshall's other idea was one of partial equilibrium. He dealt with the economy sector by sector, holding the rest of the system constant as he did so. He did not believe in economy-wide truths, holding that each industry – its techniques, its capital, its labour form, its geography – was *sui generis*. This, too, is a fundamental difference from the Austrians.

Lastly, Marshall was convinced that the Ricardo tradition that money altered the economy was correct. In other words, he differentiated, in a way that the continentals did not, monetary economics from other economics, and thought that money was a separate subject needing special analysis to explain boom and slump. This part of his teaching was mainly oral. It was the part that most interested Keynes.

This corpus of teaching was extremely powerful. It was handed on to Keynes's father, Pigou, Lord Brand, Lord Stamp, Lady Wootton, D. H. Robertson and – above all – to J. M. Keynes. By modern standards Cambridge in the 1880s and 1890s was a small university, and the embryonic Faculty of Economics was tiny. It attracted brilliant and committed young men and Marshall had an individual influence on them all, whether they went into the City, Whitehall or academic life (Keynes did all three).

Pigou succeeded Marshall. In many ways his was a bad influence; though a historian, he believed in a mathematical system, and what Marshall left untidy and allusive he made clear and, often enough, banal. His cast of mind was conservative, and he strongly influenced Robertson. Oddly enough, though Keynes is the victim of snide remarks because of his bisexuality, Pigou and Robertson, the two conservatives, were the two bachelors. (Pigou was the greater proselytiser, through his hearty climbing holidays in the Lakes.) Both Pigou and Robertson were extremely economical. Robertson, the son of a headmaster of Haileybury, then subsequently a poor parson, had a desperate fear of poverty, allied to a great belief in consols. These two were Keynes's intellectual intimates. His interests were wider, especially in logic, derived from his father, the logician, and pure philosophy with Moore and Wittgenstein. But in economics he talked to Pigou and Robertson, till both were superseded by Kahn, Sraffa and the younger Keynesians after about 1930.

Keynes swallowed all of Marshall, though he rejected two sets of doctrines developed by Pigou. One was an excessive reverence for the price system; he regarded it as a purely pragmatic matter whether or not prices were the best allocative mechanism. The other, infinitely more important, was that he followed Marshall's hints and unsystematised notions about the rate of interest and money into a rejection of the idea that capitalism tended to sustain an equilibrium rate of employment provided that wage levels were sufficiently flexible. This rejection of Say's Law, that supply creates its own demand, was the cornerstone of Keynes's theory of unemployment.

Keynes, then, was not a rebel against the Cambridge tradition, though the Cambridge tradition was insulated against continental economics. The subsequent lumping together of Marshall's careful version of the way the economy actually worked, and Walras and Menger, under the title 'neo-classic', tends to exaggerate grossly the extent to which Keynes was a radical. He had a profound sense of reverence for his forebears, not least his father, who outlived him, and his biography of Marshall was among the finest essays he ever wrote. On the other hand, together with this reverence, he had the Bloomsbury urge *épater le bourgeois*; if there were two ways of saying something, he chose the more shocking. This was partly a habit of mind and partly because he was a great and fluent stylist, with a style at once robust and rococo.

Austin Robinson once told me that Keynes wrote several thousand words a day and rarely threw any of them away. His Collected Works show that he had no need to do so. It suggests, however, what Lord Kahn and Joan Robinson have emphasised, that to search for a narrow consistency in Keynes's thought is to misunderstand his nature of working. He chose, at Marshall's prompting, to specialise in money and banking. He knew more about the City than any of his contemporaries except those, like Brand, who worked there, and Hawtrey in the Treasury. He was himself an inveterate speculator and gambler, chiefly in commodities. He loved intellectual speculation as well: he preferred the stimulus of a bright idea to the certainty of the carefully-phrased finality. It is probably this that attracted him to 'money' – i. e., the City – as a subject of study; Marshall regarded his own doctrines in this field as unfinished, while his work on industry and the market system seemed pretty final.

It is this speculative nature – the Etonian grandee, perhaps, as opposed to the Bank of England clerk's son – that made Keynes so inspiring a teacher of clever people. Champagne, quicksilver, lightning are some of the metaphors used to describe his intellectual challenge to his pupils, ·as at the Political Economy Club, which met in his rooms to read and discuss papers, the discussants being chosen by lot. (The tradition was carried on by D. H. Robertson in his icy rooms in Great Court, a frugal tea served between the paper and the discussion. (Another older tradition lingered. Marshall was a bad lecturer. We were morally obliged to attend Mr Guillebaud's lectures and protest was silenced by 'Mr Guillebaud is Marshall's nephew'.)

After the Great Depression of 1929–31, Keynes moved for a decade with a younger set, mediated through the brilliant Richard Kahn. A new, genuinely radical note arrived in Cambridge economics. Kahn, more than anyone else, was responsible for the *General Theory,* by explaining that an economy could be in equilibrium and still have massive unemployment. But another, deadlier thread had been drawn out of the fabric of Marshall's thought by Piero Sraffa. Sraffa, friend of the great Wittgenstein and of the Italian communist leader Gramsci, took Marshall's key tool of the representative firm and showed that competition and increasing returns to scale (a characteristic of large-scale industry) were incompatible. Joan Robinson developed this idea, so that the modern theory, that prices are determined not by supply and demand, but by cost plus a profit margin, was much in the air. Marshall's allegiance to the price system had been pragmatic, not *a priori.* There was no longer any intellectual reason to suppose that the price system allocated resources any better than any other system; in any particular case it was a matter of fact and judgment.

Keynes contributed to economics in many fields. His major work was on the theory of money and, eventually, on the theory of employment – what is now called macro-economics. The evidence, from Dr Eshag's study of Keynes's work on the rate of interest, and from the long correspondence (now published) with other Cambridge economists, is that Keynes's thought was deeply embedded in the Cambridge tradition. After all, he wrote the preface for the Cambridge economic handbooks, probably the most brilliant series of textbooks ever produced in the social sciences, and the series included a book by D. H. Robertson called *Money.* The differences between Keynes's approach and Robertson's were exaggerated in the heat of controversy after the appearance of the *General Theory,* but Harry Johnson's work has shown that formally the two can be reduced to very similar formulations.

This is not to deny the extreme originality of Keynes's

thought on the determination of the level of employment. On the fundamental issue, whether unemployment was due to too high a money-wage level, Pigou was on one side and Keynes on the other and it was not till Keynes had been dead for some years that Pigou announced that he had been converted to Keynes's view, a conversion that caused much wailing and weeping and remarks about senility. But the fact that even in old age Pigou could still go along with Keynes's fundamental revision of the theory of employment suggests that the Keynes innovation, though great, was well within the general corpus of Cambridge theory. That is a point of view that the Keynesians would have contested at the time, but it is clear from the preface to the French edition of the *General Theory* that Keynes himself was aware of the complexity of his own position:

> For a hundred years or longer English Political Economy has been dominated by an orthodoxy. That is not to say that an unchanging doctrine has prevailed. On the contrary. There has been a progressive evolution of the doctrine. But its presuppositions, its atmosphere, its method have remained surprisingly the same, and a remarkable continuity has been observable through all the changes. In that orthodoxy, in that continuous transition, I was brought up. I learnt it, I taught it, I wrote it. To those looking from outside I probably still belong to it. Subsequent historians of doctrine will regard this book as in essentially the same tradition. But I myself in writing it, and in other recent work which has led up to it, have felt myself to be breaking away from this orthodoxy, to be in strong reaction against it, to be escaping from something, to be gaining an emancipation.

And in the preface to the Japanese edition he makes a more explicit claim:

> Alfred Marshall, on whose *Principles of Economics* all contemporary English economists have been brought up, was at particular pains to emphasise the continuity of his thought with Ricardo's. His work largely consisted in grafting the marginal principle and the principle of substitution on to the Ricardian tradition; and his theory of output and con-

sumption as a whole, as distinct from his theory of the production and distribution of a *given* output, was never separately expounded. Whether he himself felt the need of such a theory, I am not sure. But his immediate successors and followers have certainly dispensed with it and have not, apparently, felt the lack of it. It was in this atmosphere that I was brought up. I taught these doctrines myself and it is only within the last decade that I have been conscious of their insufficiency. In my own thought and development, therefore, this book represents a reaction, a transition away from the English classical (or orthodox) tradition.

– that is, that in the ten years after Marshall's death it was the other Cambridge economists who were out of step with Marshall.

The other chief contribution that Keynes made was to policy. I do not mean by this that his ideas were usually or even occasionally adopted as a result of the minutes that he wrote in government service, or the constant flow of journalism which he kept up. It was this constant concern with the actual which differentiated his thought most dramatically from the work of other economists, which was more abstract, or more concerned, not with political economy, but with statistical series and a narrow concept of economics. His literary and journalistic work covered an enormous breadth of intellectual life, which deeply affected his economics. In this respect he was, of course, a broader man than Marshall (to imagine Marshall at the ballet is like imagining Wagner at an economics seminar).

Keynes shifted, then, from being the radical member of a Marshallian group to being the more conservative member of a younger group which was predominantly socialist, while still being heavily Marshallian. It must be said that Marshall's economic catholicity, and the sheer power of his analytical system, enabled the transition to be made with remarkably little strain. Since he believed in evidence, changing evidence could be accommodated in his theory as it could not in those more rigid systems that Hayek brought to the LSE and the refugees took to America, where they overwhelmed the native American institutionalist school, now revived by Galbraith. At any time, Keynes's break with tradition applied only to part of it; the rest he continued to embrace. He never, in print at least, faced up to the long-period consequences of his short-period analysis in the *General Theory;* these problems were left to two of his pupils, Sir Roy Harrod and Professor Joan Robinson, and to Lord Kaldor.

In the last five years of his life Keynes was reconciled with D. H. Robertson. The breach between the two men covered the crucial decade of the 1930s. The reconciliation gives some ground for thinking that Keynes returned to his more conservative stance as the country moved to the left. I doubt whether this is true. It is idle to speculate what Keynes might have said after he was dead; he had a genius for the unexpected. But we know that he strongly urged Hugh Dalton to pursue a cheap money policy, and that he supported the American loan. Both involved radical departures from orthodoxy. The breach with Robertson I had supposed to come from Keynes, who had found new friends; the correspondence now proves it was Robertson who broke with Keynes over the *General Theory*. Robertson, brilliant, brave, waspish, was deeply conservative. The sad family history of genteel poverty, the minor parsonical snobbery, the suppressed shyness all made him easy to like but hard to persevere with. He saw reds under all non--Etonian and some Etonian beds. He refused to be swept up in the enthusiasm for an untidy book like the *General Theory*.

So Keynes passed on, always tackling new problems, not particularly concerned with consistency. His intellectual heirs are also Marshallians – Kahn and Joan Robinson. But a new note, Sraffa, was introduced into the Cambridge symphony by Keynes himself, and it is Sraffa who, for fifteen years now, has superseded Keynes as the dominant influence. Keynes is praised and blamed for thoughts and actions that were not his. The great boom of 1948–70 is labelled 'Keynesian'; the great inflation of 1967 to now is labelled 'Keynesian'; the little men predicting the output of peas to the nearest kilogram for the next seventeen weeks label themselves 'Keynesian'. They are none of them anything to do with J. M. Keynes, the brilliant, affectionate, subtle mind that has been dead for thirty years. His followers have turned to other questions, as he would himself, and their answers are not necessarily his. As he would have been the first to assert, proudly, he wanted equals, not disciples.

3 The Last of the Romans

Marcello de Cecco

Through no fault of his own, but merely as a result of his being a post-Edwardian Englishman, Keynes spent one half of his adult life making history, the other half on the receiving end of it.

As a junior civil servant at the India Office, he helped to influence the lives of hundreds of millions of Indian subjects. He did so without pausing to reflect on the enormity of the fact. He had been taught that the British upper class had a natural aptitude for ruling, for making history. History-makers do not have much sense of history. They do not need it.

As a participant in the Versailles Conference, Keynes began to realise what revenge a humiliated and defeated country like Germany could meditate and then effect on the victors. He was, as is known, extremely vocal in giving vent to his fears and indignation, and, again, he was making history. In his profile of president Wilson one can detect, however, a faint realisation of the fact that a new and more powerful protagonist had appeared on the scene, the United States. And that meant a smaller role for Britain.

Finally, in the last two years of the Second World War, Keynes had to fight, and even sacrifice his life, in a vain attempt to prevent the United States from dictating over the destinies of 50 million Britons. Thus Keynes lived through the meridian age of British power, and long enough to see his own role, as an economic adviser, rotate 180 degrees, through his country's decline, from history-maker to history-taker. His economic plans reflect this progression.

His formative years impinged heavily on his later writings. He never considered the problems of supply as interesting, on the very good assumption that Britain had even too much of it. He remained convinced till the last that only the dismal

18

mediocrity of politicians, the shortsightedness of entrepreneurs, the imbecility of the rentier and incompetence and greed of bankers prevented Britain from reaching an age of plenty, a new and lasting renaissance.

The sense that everything was possible, and within reach, if only ... was steeped in a deep knowledge of the economic conditions of early twentieth-century Britain. The British economist did well to ignore the supply side. So much productive capacity had been created over two centuries of industrialisation; so much capital had been accumulated in financial form; so many imperial markets were captive and ready to take anything the British found fit to produce. Any malfunctioning of the British economy had thus to be necessarily due to internal rather than external causes. Keynes belonged to a fortunate group of British economists who could not only take supply for granted, but also consider the British economy plus the Empire as a closed, self-contained, system. Naturally enough, they looked, for the causes of any malfunctioning, at the very heart of the British economy, the financial system.

Again, it was a correct perspective. That Keynes was obsessed with all things financial is clear from the very first pages of his Collected Works. In the Britain of his time, however, it would have been impossible not to be. So clear a hegemony of finance over every other form of economic activity has never existed anywhere else. With respect to the British manufacturing sector, the City always remained almost an offshore island. In the early years of Keynes's adulthood, industrial shares were a small and unimportant part of the Stock Exchange, whose main activity was to deal with the myriad of foreign loans, floated especially on behalf of foreign public authorities. It was a Stock Exchange dominated by the coupon, rather than by dividends and capital gains, as it is today. The City's other main financial activities included the discounting and accepting of bills, these being the speciality of, respectively, discount houses and merchant banks. Over the lot presided the Bank of England, linked directly to the merchant banks through its Court of Directors, whose members came from those banks.

It must be emphasised that, to most traders and manufacturers from the industrial North, the financial community of

London had always been foreign; the City was a place to put one's spare money, but not a place where one could borrow either long-term capital or short-term finance. A provincial banking system had thus arisen and prospered, to cater to the needs of the manufacturers and domestic traders, and it was managed by people very different from the merchant bankers and other City gents. They were either self-made men or the descendants of small provincial bankers, and they had not gone through the public-school system, where the merchant bankers were educated and where they mixed with future politicians, administrators and dons, forming almost tribal links, and developing a sense of caste loyalty. The provincial bankers (who were then called joint stock bankers) were not part of this charmed circle, where power was monopolised in the hands of people who, however, needed the money of the joint stock bankers to conduct most of their affairs. This made for an uneasy relationship between the joint stock bankers, clamouring for a say, to which they thought their huge spare cash entitled them, in the financial and monetary policy of their country, and the charmed circle, feeling the greatest possible disgust for these vulgar upstarts who wanted a share in what the merchant bankers thought was their natural monopoly.

This running battle between the City and the joint stock bankers caused great trouble for the British financial system. Its fierce manifestations during the crisis of July–August 1914 fascinated Keynes. Typically for a young man who had been at Eton and Cambridge and had sat, like young Jesus among the wise men, on the Royal Commission on Indian Currency and Finance, Keynes took the side of the City's inner sanctum. He did, however, recognise with great clarity that the feud between the two groups was the source of most of the problems that the British financial system had gone, and was going, through.

Through these early encounters with British financial power, however, Keynes began to develop the feeling that the financial system held the British economy to ransom, that it had replaced the aristocratic landowners in exacting an extortionate rent from the manufacturing sector, giving it a permanent propensity towards deflation and unemployment. It is fascinating to trace the emergence of this theme, from the status of a feeling to a fully articulated theory, in Keynes's own writings. It is a theme as central to his work as that of expectations and speculation, and as the conviction that irrational behaviour is as common, widespread, and natural as is behaviour based on the neo-classical model of individual utility maximisation.

If one looks at them carefully, Keynes's main analytical works, the *Treatise on Money* and the *General Theory*, explain through what forces, mechanisms and circuits the richest economy in the world was reduced to working at half-steam. These forces, mechanisms and circuits had, in his opinion, all to do with the peculiarly infelicitous mingling of a huge rentier class and a huge financial system. The interactions of these two protagonists of a century of British economic history were at the centre of Keynes's analytic stage. He was fascinated by a circuit that managed to link savings to financial assets, and to exclude real assets, therefore investment. The interaction of savers and the City was, to him, an almost closed circuit, a vicious circle from which the British economy could not escape by itself, because everything within that circuit worked according to a logic of almost perverse rationality. This is perhaps the greatest of Keynes's achievements. He showed how a system could get into underemployment equilibrium, and stay there, just by respecting the same golden rules as had made the system work at full-employment level in a previous age. Once the rentier class and the financial system had reached a certain critical size, the same interaction between them which had made Britain great plunged it into a permanent slump. Keynes's achievement was to show how a physiology can become a pathology without much structural change.

The reason why this had happened is rather simple to explain. The British had been savers and bankers to the whole world for a crucial fifty years. This had meant a gigantic development of saving and banking, which, relative to other functions performed by the domestic economy, had become enormous. With the relapse of the world economy into post-war stagnation, and with the development of saving and banking in other countries, the British found themselves with too much capacity for saving and for financial intermediation, compared to the capacity to invest and consume of their domestic economy. British savers and bankers were like great eagles compelled, by world events, to fly in a small cage, Britain. There was a need to scale them down, and a need to prop up domestic investment and consumption, to re-establish some sort of balance.

There are many other things that matter in Keynes's main works, but I think his masterpiece was his translation of the most important features of British economic history into economic theory. He managed to give theoretical clothes to all the aspects of British economic life that mattered most. His theory is not a stylisation of facts: it is a complete picture, a photograph in which the likeness of the actors is not sacrificed at all. Everything in the *Treatise* and in the *General Theory* is derived from the British experience: the assumptions, the protagonists, the stage, the action. How else could we explain the peculiarly central role of money, and of fixed-interest securities, the peculiar absence of investment, of common shares, of anything relating to capital accumulation? How else could we explain the divorce between savers and investors, and the completely passive role labour plays in the action?

Let us be frank. Keynes thought he had buried Ricardian economics, but in his works, particularly in the *General Theory*, he was only praising it. Labour had been marginal in Ricardo's work, which was an analysis of how the outcome of the fight between landowners and industrial capitalists for a share of the surplus determined the rate of capital accumulation. Keynes substituted the financier for the landowner and focused on the level of unemployment (rather than on the rate of capital accumulation) resulting from the same fight. Full employment in an age of plenty was to him what capital accumulation in an age of scarcity was to Ricardo: the premier instrument of social stabilisation. For both Ricardo and Keynes the workers were altogether secondary. They were mere clay in the hands of the real protagonists of economic life. But they were capable of revolt against a system which they did not influence, but which shaped their lives completely.

Both Keynes and Ricardo lived in troubled social times. In both periods workers had been rebelling. Ricardo thought that cheap food – i.e. the abolition of the Corn Laws and of the agricultural rents' stranglehold on the economy – was the solution. Keynes thought that, in the existing conditions of the

British economy, cheap money would be the equivalent of cheap food, and that, if even that was not enough, direct investment by the state would do the job.

Both Ricardo and Keynes were enlightened conservatives. Both were advocating, like the Sicilian Prince Fabrizio in *The Leopard*, that everything change, so that everything might remain the same, and gave the prescriptions that would permit the miracle. Their prescriptions were applied, and the miracle happened: the British social and political system survived, almost unchanged, though 200 years of economic revolution.

Keynes was less fortunate in securing an appropriate international context for his domestic remedies. Here the crude realities of the American power monopoly were too strong for intelligence alone to overcome and Keynes the history-maker was a victim of Britain's radical enfeeblement.

Between 1941 and 1944, he exhausted his physical resources in the attempt to construct an international economic environment which would help Britain to adjust to a lesser role. He was convinced that the United States had become a huge agent of world-wide deflation, as its external accounts always presented a structural surplus on both trade and capital. The only way to stem the deflationary tide was by setting up an international clearing union (ICU) which would create international liquidity and lend it to deficit countries, thus helping them to make the adjustment less painful in terms of employment. He tried, in this way, to re-create a pure Ricardian international payments system, where the specie flow mechanism was replaced by ICU liquidity, and which would exclude the destructive short-term capital flows that had made international economic relations so bitter in the inter-war period.

It was, of course, a losing battle. The Americans were not interested. New York banks were set upon replacing the City of London and were all in favour of free international capital flows. They were also in favour of higher interest rates and of an end to cheap money. They rightly thought the Keynesian clearing union would keep world demand (which was largely demand for US-made commodities) too high, stifle capital flows, and prevent the resurrection of monetary policy as the premier instrument of short-term economic policy. Besides, the US could not tolerate that the purchasing power that a

Keynesian world bank would create, which would end up largely as purchasing power on American goods, should be outside US control. As they paid the piper, they wanted to call the tune – which meant *ad hoc* bilateral negotiations, between the US and borrowing countries, as a powerful tool to 'convert' reluctant, dirigistic European countries to the principle of free trade.

So Keynes lost his last battle. He began life as a Roman, he ended it as a mere Italian; too late, however, to acquire the lucid bitterness of Niccoló Machiavelli.

4 Two Critics of Keynes: Friedman and Hayek

Peter Lilley

For most of the last forty years the average student of economics in Britain or America has been shielded from any systematic critique of the Keynesian system. He is, of course, given an account – often little more than a caricature – of the obscurantist resistance put up by die-hard 'classical' economists to the original Keynesian revolution. Indeed, part of the appeal of the Keynesian system is that it presents itself as revolutionary and nonconformist whilst in fact being thoroughly established. Thus it satisfies the twin but conflicting desires of most young men – to rebel and to conform. But students have not, at least until recently, been taught about the genuinely nonconformist schools of thought which have continued to develop detailed criticisms of the Keynesian orthodoxy.

This rather unacademic taboo certainly still operated at Cambridge a decade ago. I stumbled on its existence only because I happened to be too obtuse to grasp the sophisticated Keynesian justification for state control of the economy. My supervisor therefore reluctantly introduced me to some authors who would help me 'to express my outmoded prejudices in rigorous academic form'. But I was first required to swear not to tell anyone that I had been advised to read Friedman and his Chicago colleagues! Thus only under a veil of secrecy could one even discover the existence of an alternative to the Keynesian approach.

The existence of a second, distinct (though overlapping) anti-Keynesian school – the Austrian tradition under von Mises and its present doyen, Professor Hayek – was an even more closely guarded secret.

In recent years the Anglo-American academic establishment has at last been forced to grant diplomatic recognition to

25

both the Chicago and Austrian schools. Not only have they failed to wither away in academic isolation, but they show every sign of flourishing at a time when the established Keynesian doctrine is proving theoretically sterile and politically inoperable.

Before this reversal of fortunes can be understood it is helpful to understand why the Keynesian hegemony came about. The original victory was amazingly rapid compared with most intellectual revolutions. Keynes published his *General Theory* in 1936. By the outbreak of war it was firmly established and opposition within the academic establishment had virtually ceased.

The reasons for this sweeping advance are doubtless manifold. However, the *General Theory* did not catch on because of its lucidity and simplicity. It possesses neither characteristic. Professor Samuelson, a leading Keynesian whose best selling textbook has done much to spread the Keynesian system, wrote of the *General Theory*, 'It is a badly written book, poorly organised; any layman who, beguiled by the author's previous reputation, bought the book was cheated of his five shillings. It is not well suited for classroom use. It is arrogant, bad tempered, polemical and not overly generous in its acknowledgements. It abounds in mares' nests and confusions. . . . In short, it is a work of genius' (*The Development of Economic Thought,* ed. H. W. Spiegel (Wiley, 1952), p. 767).

Even acknowledging that genius lay beneath the obscurity and confusions, it is amazing that people perceived it so speedily.

One major factor underlying the success of the *General Theory* was that it provided, or purported to provide, a way out of a very uncomfortable dilemma. Contemporary economics taught the economics profession something they did not want to believe – namely, that the higher the real wage stipulated by workers the fewer would be employed. This implied that unemployment could be cured if trades unions permitted workers in the hardest-hit industries to accept lower wages. Yet academics, being comfortably off and securely employed, felt acutely embarrassed at advising workers to accept lower wages. Keynes explicity recognised this embarrassment: 'A classical economist may sympathise with labour in refusing a cut in its money-wage . . . but scientific integrity forces him to declare that this refusal is nevertheless at the bottom of the trouble' (*General Theory*, p. 16).

In the *General Theory* Keynes sought to show that rigid wages were not the cause of, and wage cuts not the cure for, unemployment. He claimed to have constructed a general theory, of which classical economic theory was just a special case valid only at full employment. Small wonder that economists should lap up with enthusiasm a book which claimed to show them how to salvage both their consciences and their existing economic expertise.

To claim to have discovered such a theory does not necessarily mean that it exists or is true. Indeed Keynes's disciples have been arguing about what his theory *is* for several decades (which may cast doubt on its existence), though they have never doubted its truth! Incidentally, this lengthy exegesis has finally generated some sort of consensus among Keynesians that, in the words of Leijonhufvud, 'his "General Theory" is but a special case of the classical theory obtained by imposing certain restrictive assumptions on the latter'. In short, the book which aimed to reduce classical economics to a special case of a more general theory has suffered the reverse fate. That the economics profession should nonetheless value Keynes's contribution so highly may in part be explained by Harry Johnson's quip that 'the effort required to open the oyster led those who were successful to overvalue the pearl within' ('The General Theory after 25 years', in Johnson's *On Economics and Society*).

The very obscurity of the *General Theory* was one of its strengths. Disciples could believe it contained a revolutionary alternative to classical economics. Critics could be declared to have misunderstood what Keynes 'really meant'. However, Keynes did subsequently define the elements that *he* considered to be crucial to his theory (see his 'The General Theory of Employment', *Quarterly Journal of Economics*, LI (1937)).

The twin pillars of his system were his explanations of what determines the two components of effective demand – consumption and investment.

Consumption is determined by a stable 'psychological law . . . that when aggregate income increases, consumption expenditure will also increase but to a somewhat lesser extent'.

Keynes emphasised that this apparently banal 'psychological law was of the utmost importance in the development of my own thought'.

This 'law' has two contentious implications. First, if real incomes are tending to rise, consumption will tend to lag behind; hence, unless investment expands to absorb the growing savings, total effective demand will not grow rapidly enough to keep everyone employed. Thus there may be an in-built tendency for unemployment to rise as the economy gets richer. Second, Keynes's consumption function assumes consumers to be mechanical and irrational. Their savings are determined purely by current income, not by expected future income or accumulated savings.

Keynes's second pillar, investment, depends on the interest rate, which is determined by 'liquidity preference'. 'Liquidity preference' is a measure of people's desire to hold their assets in liquid form (money) at the sacrifice of interest yielded by less liquid instruments (bonds). When people were apprehensive they would, according to Keynes, have a greater liquidity preference; i.e. they would prefer to hold money until the interest rate increased to restore a balance between the supply of money and the supply of bonds. The higher interest rate would then reduce investment. Conversely, increasing confidence would reduce liquidity preference, lower interest rates and encourage investment. Unfortunately, according to Keynes, the collective 'liquidity preference' (which in modern jargon is an aspect of the 'demand function for money') is highly unstable. There is, Keynes believed, no rational way of knowing what the future holds. So people tend to follow the collective mood, which sways irrationally from gloom to elation, and their demand for money changes correspondingly.

The Friedmanite critique of Keynesianism has taken Keynes at his word and concentrated its fire on these twin pillars of his system – the consumption function and the demand for money (liquidity preference).

Keynes had stated that his 'consumption function' was a 'fundamental psychological law, upon which we are entitled to depend both *a priori* from our knowledge of human nature and from the detailed facts of *experience*'. However, Friedman and the pre-Keynesian economic theory to which he remained attached had a different view of human nature and he set about showing that his view generated a consumption function more in accord with the 'detailed facts of experience'. The classical view of economic man is that he is, on the whole and on average, a rational being who attempts to make the most of the opportunities open to him. A rational man will divide his income between spending and saving in the light of his expected future income and his existing assets. This is in marked contrast to Keynesian man, whose consumption and saving are determined almost exclusively and quite mechanically by past income.

If the Keynesian view is correct, two predictions follow: first, rich people will save a higher proportion of their income than will poor people, and, second, if society as a whole gets richer, the proportion of national income saved will tend to rise. The first prediction was soon found to be perfectly true. However, Simon Kuznets, Friedman's colleague at Chicago, showed the second prediction to be false. Savings have been a fairly constant ratio of national income in the long term.

Friedman's achievement was to explain these two apparently contradictory findings and show them to be compatible with his own theory of rational consumer behaviour. He realised that snapshot studies of savings patterns in one period concealed the fact that some people (authors, stockbrokers, farmers) have volatile incomes. In years when their income is high they will appear among the rich and will, *if they are rational*, save a disproportionate amount for lean years. Those who are having a bad year will appear among the poor and will draw on past savings, so their current rate of savings will appear negative. Thus much of the apparent difference between the savings habits of rich and poor, which had seemed to confirm Keynes's mechanical consumption function, could be explained as a rational response to volatile incomes.

Friedman elaborated his findings into a consumption function which fitted the data quite well (by no means perfectly, but far better than Keynes's). This consumption function differs from Keynes's in that the spectre of under-consumption in the long term as savings rise faster than investment appears decidedly less likely.

Having demolished one pillar of the Keynesian system, Friedman set about the other: the instability of the demand for money. In a massive work of scholarship Friedman reconstructed the *Monetary History of the United States, 1867–1960*. He showed therein that, on the whole, people's willingness to hold money balances has been remarkably stable. Moreover, the main periods of economic instability have been associated with erratic movements in the *supply* of money – which is determined by the monetary authorities. For example, the Great Depression of 1929–33 was accompanied (and in Friedman's view made so severe and prolonged) by a contraction of no less than one-third in the US money supply. The lesson is clear: whereas Keynesian theory suggests that the herd instinct of businessmen causes booms and slumps, Friedman's examination of the facts suggests that governments are the major source of instability.

Subsequently Friedman and other members of the Chicago school began to test quantitative equations for the demand for money. They are satisfied that the results show demand for money to be a reasonably stable function of a number of variables. Apart from suggesting that individuals are more rational about the form in which they hold their assets than Keynes believed, these money-demand functions provide an alternative to the Keynesian multiplier for forecasting short-term economic movements. Often the two techniques result in identical forecasts, but when they have differed the monetarist approach has proved more frequently correct.

The Austrian critique of the Keynesian system is in a sense far more fundamental. Whereas Friedman merely denies the empirical truth of Keynes's main postulates, Hayek rejects the whole Keynesian approach. Consequently the Austrian attack is to some extent directed at Friedman as well as at Keynes.

Hayek's first objection to the Keynesian approach is its 'conceptual realism' (the tendency to ascribe a real existence to arbitrary statistical aggregates such as consumption, the wage level, and capital). To Hayek, the wage level is as unreal as a mediaeval 'humour'. It is simply the statistical average of all individual wages. This average cannot enter into actual economic relationships. Only individual wage rates can do that. This may sound pedantic. But constant reference to 'the wage level' has obscured from a generation of economists the fact that unemployment may exist because the *structure* of relative wages is wrong, even though the *average* 'wage level' may be 'correct'. We still suffer from this type of thinking, manifested in such policies as the £6 wage increase. Blanket implementation of this, regardless of the supply-and-demand situation in different occupations, is undoubtedly pricing some workers out of jobs even though shortages of labour persist elsewhere.

Hayek's second criticism derives from his total scepticism about the existence of quantitative functional relationships in economics. The behaviour of myriads of individuals in a constantly changing society is too complex to be encapsulated in an arithmetic formula. Thus Keynes was not merely wrong in his formulation of the consumption function, but foolish to believe that any fixed relationship between consumption and income should exist. And Friedman, too, will find his consumption and money demand functions need constant modification to accord with changing circumstances. Obviously, Hayek's attitude destroys the rationale of most modern econometric work, which helps explain why it is unpopular in the profession!

Hayek's third critique of Keynes is directed at his capital theory. Because Keynes treats capital as an homogenous substance, he ignores its complex interlocking structure – remove one component (say a steelworks) and many other components (for instance, the iron and coal mines and steel fabricating plants) become useless. The market can build up such a properly co-ordinated capital structure only if the market signals (prices and interest rates) give a correct indication of the availability of resources. Keynes's recommendation that interest rates be artificially depressed to stimulate employment ignores this. Low interest rates indicate a cheap and plentiful supply of savings. Entrepreneurs will therefore initiate mutually complementary projects requiring much money and time to complete. This will indeed stimulate employment. But wages and consumption will therefore rise, diverting resources away from capital investment. The entrepreneurs will then find their supply of cheap credit choked off and incomplete capital projects left on their hands. Moreover, even if some plants are completed with the now reduced supply of savings, they are of diminished value without the expected complementary plants originally envisaged by the market. A painful period inevitably ensues during which firms are liquidated and their plant and labour is reallocated to form a viable and properly co-ordinated structure of production. The results of Keynesian cheap-money policies are therefore boom and bust.

The Austrian school therefore differs from both Keynes and Friedman in its interpretation of the Great Depression (see Murray Rothbart's book of that name). Whereas Keynes pins the blame on the irrational herd instinct of businessmen and Friedman blames the Federal Reserve Board for allowing the money supply to contract, the Austrians blame the massive, unsustainable credit expansion during the 1920s, and believe that the resultant crisis was perpetuated by attempts to *resist* the liquidation of disco-ordinated capital projects.

Arising in part from this analysis of the consequences of unwise monetary policy, comes Hayek's most recent departure from both Keynes and Friedman. Whereas Keynes depicts the role of monetary policy as being to offset the instability of liquidity preference, and Friedman that believes that its role should be to stabilise the growth of money supply, Hayek recommends that government relinquish its control of money altogether! He believes that the legal-tender laws which oblige us to use government currency should be abolished, leaving people free to choose the currency they prefer. This would prevent governments from distorting the economy by Keynesian cheap-money policies and would be a more effective discipline than Friedman's monetary rule.

If proof were needed that Keynes's critics have regained the intellectual upper hand, it is that such formerly *outré* ideas can now be discussed in Cambridge common rooms without fear of reprisal!

5 The Political Meaning of the Keynesian Revolution

ROBERT SKIDELSKY

Did Keynes help save capitalist democracy or did he nudge it towards its doom? A good Marxist answer would be that he did both, and in this case the Marxists are right. Keynes found a way of keeping capitalist democracy working, but only by weakening further the long-run conditions for its survival. Hence our ambivalent attitude towards Keynes today. Recognising in him the author alike of our economic health and sickness we don't quite know what attitude to take. The Master himself is still largely immune from attack; Keynesians or 'pseudo-Keynesians' are fair game. But this really will not do. We cannot so easily separate Keynes from his consequences, from the style of thought and order of priorities to which his revolution gave rise. To say that had he lived he would have remained more flexible than his disciples is true but trivial. There was no more chance of his becoming 'pre-Keynesian' again than there was of Copernicus once more becoming a flat-earther. One has to take Keynes with the Keynesians.

Undoubtedly Keynes was a good thing. He advanced human knowledge in economics. As a result – and this is where his political significance lies – he gave capitalist democracy a programme on which to fight back against fascism and communism. This programme, however imperfectly applied, has been fantastically successful. Although, as we can now see, it was inadequate, time was gained to tame both demons, so that the chances of a benign order beyond capitalist democracy are much brighter today than they were forty years ago.

This last point is often forgotten by those who harp on the admitted weaknesses of the present economic dispensation. Max Beloff recently wrote in *New Society*, 'In my view, there is little doubt but that the individual who (perhaps unwittingly) most seriously damaged the interests of his native country was Lord Keynes.' I like the 'perhaps'; but what really does Professor Beloff mean? Is he claiming that there was some non-Keynesian way of overcoming the slump of the 1930s, or preventing future slumps arising, which would have served capitalist democracy better? Or that there was some democratic way of tackling Britain's problems which did not involve Keynesian-type intervention? If so, these alternatives should be spelled out. Remember that the inter-war years were the time when liberal systems toppled like ninepins, largely because of uncontrollable economic fluctuations. Under what kind of system would we be living today had those fluctuations been allowed to continue? It is against this background, rather than against some individualist ideal, that the Keynesian achievement must be measured.

The way Keynes set out to tackle the economic problem reflected his personal and political values – a point which economists sometimes forget. He called himself an 'immoralist', but was never a social or political radical. He refused to join the Labour Party, stating quite frankly that 'the class war will find me on the side of the educated bourgeoisie'. Keynes's ideal was aesthetic, not moral – something misunderstood by A. L. Rowse, who tried to convert him to socialism in the early 1930s. The charge against capitalism, therefore, was not general, but particular; its failure to realise the abundance which modern technology made possible, an abundance that was the necessary condition for experiments in new styles of living. This failure could be remedied by certain limited changes. Keynes insisted on the need to distinguish 'the Agenda of Government from the non-Agenda'. The important thing for government 'is not to do things which individuals are doing already . . . but to do those things which at present are not done at all'. The chief economic fault of individualistic capitalism was its failure to provide full employment. No one was responsible for keeping demand as a whole sufficiently high to provide employment for all those seeking work. This fact suggested the economic agenda for modern government.

Its task should be to secure an 'aggregate volume of output corresponding to full employment', leaving the market to allocate resources and rewards as hitherto. Keynes thought this objective might require a 'somewhat comprehensive socialisation if investment'. What he appears to have meant by this vague and alarming phrase was no more than that the state should be prepared to augment private investment sufficiently to produce full employment. Whether, or to what extent, it would *have* to do so, only experience would show. Beyond this, the state should use the taxation system to redistribute income 'in a way likely to raise the propensity to consume', while allowing for 'significant inequalities of incomes and wealth'. Thus the two main actors in the Keynesian system were to be the government and the market, dividing the labour of economic life between them.

The precise economic rationale for focusing on aggregate demand, rather than on supply, need not detain us here. Nevertheless, it had such important political implications that it is difficult to believe that the direction of Keynes's inquiry was not influenced by political considerations. First, his view that, if demand was right, supply would look after itself undermined not just Say's Law (which said the opposite), but also the socialist case for public ownership, which rested on the inefficiency and injustice of the allocative mechanism under capitalism. It suggested, in fact, an alternative economic strategy to the one outlined by the Labour Party at that time. Secondly, it avoided having to choose between capital and labour. Keeping demand buoyant would simultaneously underwrite high profits, full employment and rising wages, thus eliminating or at least easing the conflict over the distribution of wealth. Thirdly, the decision for macro-economic, as opposed to micro-economic, intervention was a decision for indirect and general, as opposed to direct and detailed, economic control by government; for a 'managed' rather than a 'commanded' economy. Fiscal and monetary leverage by government could be reconciled with economic free will by individuals and groups. In this, Keynes was quite consciously seeking an alternative to dictatorship. The authoritarian state systems, he wrote in the *General Theory* (he must have had Germany, Italy, Russia and Japan in mind), 'seek to solve the problem of unemployment at the expense of efficiency and freedom. It is certain that the world will not much longer tolerate the unemployment which ... is associated ... with

present-day capitalistic individualism. But it may be possible
by a right analysis of the problem to cure the disease while
preserving efficiency and freedom. . . .'

The reference to Germany and Russia reminds us of the
chief alternative 'cures' for the economic disease then on offer.
Fascism is today so discredited that it is generally forgotten
that it was then a rapidly expanding political force. Its attrac-
tion was twofold. It promised an anti-socialist solution to the
crisis of capitalism; and it offered a political critique of
liberalism's ineffectiveness in face of crisis which seemed to fit
the experience of the Depression. Moreover, practice confirmed theory. It is now increasingly recognised that Hitler's was
the only New Deal that actually succeeded in eliminating unemployment. Roosevelt's certainly didn't. There were 15
million Americans out of work when he took office in March
1933. There were still 11 million four years later and the
economy properly recovered only with rearmament and war.
The reason was that budget deficits remained far too small to
plug the shortfall in private investment: the stimulating effect
of fiscal policy was greater in 1931, when Hoover was president, than in any of the pre-1940 Roosevelt years. The
Swedish New Deal is also largely a myth. Unemployment
dropped from 30 per cent in 1933 to 11 per cent in 1938,
but mainly because exports revived. Public works employed
only a small fraction of the unemployed; the impact of fiscal
measures was negligible. Discussion of whether Sweden's New
Deal was most influenced by Keynes, Lloyd George, Wicksell
or Marx is now seen as an attempt to explain an event which
did not occur. The significance of all this is that capitalist
democracy had not found an answer to economic fluctuations
by the late 1930s, and was therefore vulnerable to any system
which had, or said it had.

The other ideology on offer was socialism. This was not the
'democratic socialism' which, with Keynes's help, has been
evolved since the war; but one much more Marxist, and also
heavily influenced by Stalinist Russia. In Britain, the Labour
Party emerged from the Depression with a heavily non-Keynesian analysis of its causes. Rising unemployment was the consequence of substituting machines for men in producing goods
(Ricardo's 'strong case' taken over by Marx). Technological
unemployment was therefore inevitable. What was needed

was a combination of public ownership and socialist planning
to translate capitalist unemployment 'into new leisure for the
people by shortening the working life' (Arthur Greenwood).
Moreover, the Labour Left wanted this programme of industrial reorganisation to be carried out by means of an
Enabling Act, empowering a Labour government to legislate
by Orders in Council, to avoid parliamentary obstruction.
Underlying such attitudes was a deep belief in the imminent
collapse of liberal capitalism which gripped practically the
whole left-wing intelligentsia. In a number of influential
books, John Strachey denied that capitalism could save itself
either by cutting the wage bill (the orthodox remedy) or by
raising it (the Keynesian one). The first would produce a crisis
of 'realisation'; the second a crisis of profitability. In so far as
the Labour Party was not gripped by such ideas, it had little
to offer beyond the failing nostrums of capitalism's own
spokesmen. It was only in the later 1930s that a number of
younger socialists, like Douglas Jay, started to work out a
social democratic programme in Keynesian terms. The attitude of the Left was not much different in any of those countries which still preserved free institutions.

Thus capitalist democracy had no relevant philosophy of
government to put up against its critics. Keynes provided it
with one. It would be too much to say that by doing so he 'saved' capitalism, even temporarily. That was done by a combination of Keynesian ideas, the Second World War, and the
Allied victory in the war, leading to American 'underwriting'
of the free-world economy. The Keynesian Revolution was a
necessary, but not sufficient, condition for the libertarian
prosperity of the post-war years. The Second World War was
doubly important. First, it provided the laboratory for testing
out the new theories of economic management. Secondly, it
created the social consensus for which Keynesianism proved
the ideal ideology, promising, as I have suggested earlier,
benefits to all groups including government and bureaucracy.
(One should perhaps add that the power balance between
capital and labour was just about right for an ideology neutral
between the two.) But, without the existence of an appropriate
set of ideas, the post-war opportunities could have vanished as
easily as they did after 1918; an illustration of the truth that,
even when the times are ripe for a certain development, an ap-

propriate consciousness is still required to realise it. The Keynesian Revolution in economics provided that consciousness.

What then went wrong? What grounds have we for supposing that the Keynesian Revolution was a transitional stage rather than a stable state? There are, I suggest, two main grounds. One involves the first actor in the Keynesian system, the government. The other involves the second actor, the market.

Keynes overestimated the possibility of rational economic management by democratic government. Hayek thought Keynesian government would be too strong for democratic health. It has turned out to be too weak – too much penetrated by, dependent on, or at the mercy of, outside forces to be able to make its economic will prevail. This 'overloading', to use the current jargon, threatens democracy by saddling democratic governments with a cumulative burden of failure.

Keynes's own political expectations emerge quite clearly in the debate on the gold standard in the 1920s. According to the Cunliffe Report, the great merit of the pre-1914 gold standard was that it was politician-proof. Only when gold reserves went up could the note issue be expanded; when they went down, the quantity of notes went down as well. The system, in other words, imposed an automatic check on any inflationary increase in the money supply. When Keynes advocated, in its place, a 'managed' currency, the Treasury asked him pertinently how he would prevent inflation. His answer, in effect, was: by the exercise of responsible intelligence. Sir Roy Harrod rightly remarks that 'Keynes . . . deemed England a sufficiently mature country for it to be possible to assume that the authorities . . . would not indulge in an orgy of feckless note issues'. But an alternative hypothesis was possible and, as it has turned out, more realistic; which is that, once economic life became a matter for continuous political decision, economic rationality (however defined) would be subordinated to political demands through the auction for votes of a competitive political system. As early as 1931, the May Committee, more famous for its many stupidities than for its occasional nuggets of sense, noted realistically that universal suffrage and rising expectations had 'heavily loaded the dice in favour of expenditure' as the 'disappointment of many hopes in the economic sphere' intensified demands for 'improvement from political action'. The view that Keynesian government has lost control over economic policy seems closer to experience than the view popular in some quarters that government could control the money supply if it wanted to. If that is so, why has it not done so? As long as Sir Keith Joseph (for example) continues to believe that since the war 'governments in this country have had unprecedented power over economic life', he will be unable to answer this question. Responsibility yes; power no.

The other main weakness in the Keynesian system has arisen from the role it assigned to the market. Keynes's division of labour between government and market was never as theoretically, or practically, stable as he supposed. Governments have been drawn inevitably, and I think irreversibly, into the micro-economic sphere, from which Keynesian economics promised to keep them. For this there are a number of reasons.

The idea that, if demand is right, supply will look after itself was particularly delusive for an economy, such as Britain's, suffering from structural obsolescence, and fed the natural inclination of 'overloaded' post-war British governments to avoid making choices about Britain's future. Another fact of universal importance has been the growth of what Galbraith has called the 'planning system' within the so-called market sector of modern economies. Industrial concentration, and with it the power of big corporations to plan their markets, have blunted the edge of traditional Keynesian fiscal and monetary instruments, facing governments with the choice of either abdicating or superseding private by public planning. Finally, Keynesian policy has itself accelerated the growing rigidity of the economic system which makes planning necessary. For example, systemic 'cost-push' inflation would be impossible without the public commitment to full-employment output. That commitment thus forces governments to act directly on wages and prices, rather than allowing the power of employers and unions to be broken by bankruptcy and unemployment. In these ways, Keynesian governments have been drawn inexorably into economic planning to compensate for the decay of the 'disciplines of the market' produced in part by their own policies. This has upset the original Keynesian balance between government and market forces; at the same time the relative failure of democratic governments to plan successfully (for example, the repeated failures of wage–price policies) has further weakened their credibility.

In these ways, the political economy of Keynes is coming unstuck. His assumptions about what government needed to do were more valid for his day than they are for ours. With Britain's imperial markets still captive, planning for modernisation was less important. With middle-class hegemony still secure, working-class pressure was inevitably less clamant. With business and labour still relatively unorganised, the mandarins of the Treasury and the Bank were freer to make policy as they pleased. That economic life needs to be anchored once more in 'economic reality' is common ground. The sole question is on what basis. I, for one, feel certain it will be on a post-Keynesian, not pre-Keynesian, one.

6 Can Democracy Manage an Economy?

SAMUEL BRITTAN

One of the great growth industries of the English-speaking world is the exegesis of the writings of John Maynard Keynes. What exactly did Keynes say? When did he say it? Who were his precursors? What did he really mean? What should he have meant? What would he be saying if he were alive today? Anyone who finds these questions too arid will be able to find relief in the stream of new insights and revelations into the life of the great man and his significance for the era in which he lived. As a twentieth-century subject for life-and-times hagiography, he joins the select company of Freud, Mahler, Wittgenstein and a very few others.

I enjoy a good wallow as much as anyone else. But it is an interesting reflection on the would-be scientific standing of economics that exponents of rival theories think it important to find chapter and verse for their views in Keynes – which they always can, for like most such figures he said a great many different things. Can one imagine the protagonists in a controversy in modern physics trying to advance their views by showing that they were implicit in some obscure passage in Einstein, and their opponents replying either that this was a misunderstanding or that it was all really said much better by Isaac Newton (the Adam Smith of physics)?

But if there is one aspect of Keynes which unquestionably dates him, it is his attitude to the democratic process. In his economic writings he was concerned with the extent to which the pursuit of self-interest in the market place did or did not promote the general interest. But it never occurred to him to see the political process as a market place, governed by the self-interest of politicians, officials and voters. He took it for granted that decision would ultimately be made by a small group of the educated bourgeoisie, who were inspired by a dis-

interested concern for the public good. He assumed that
wrong decisions were taken out of intellectual error or, at
worst, narrowness of vision; and that if the correct ideas were
promulgated with sufficient clarity and vigour they would
eventually win the day.

These characteristics can be illustrated by the present-day
arguments between those economists who call themselves
Keynesian and those who call themselves monetarists. The
first, most highly publicised, is the importance of changes in
the money supply in influencing the economy. Keynes himself
avoided an entrenched position on this issue and would almost
certainly have been prepared to adjust his views in the light of
evidence and logical argument. He would surely have seen
(indeed, probably did see somewhere in his writings) the ab-
surdity of regarding interest rates as a guide to monetary
policy in an era of chronic inflation, when the high interest
rates about which the business community, the Tribune
Group and the home-owners lobby join forces to complain,
are heavily negative in real terms.

But a second and much more fundamental argument is
whether demand management of any kind, whether through
monetary means or through the budget, is destabilising and
actually aggravates the booms and slumps it is meant to cure.
The issue is only in part technical. Those monetarists who
follow Milton Friedman believe that we should have a much
more stable economic environment if government did not adjust the controls so often and contented themselves with a
moderate steady annual growth of the money supply and a
budget calculated to balance at high-employment levels of
business activity.

This approach is not in the spirit of Keynes at all. It is easy
to imagine Keynes pointing out the perverse effect of would-be
stabilisation measures. But the idea of abandoning discretionary management and going by fixed, preordained rules
was entirely foreign to his temperament. Both in personal and
in public life he had an unquenchable faith in men's ability to
work out directly the effect of each of their actions and behave
in good faith. In contrast to David Hume, he was an 'act
utilitarian' rather than a 'rule utilitarian'.

It is, however, a third argument between Keynes and the
monetarists which most directly challenges Keynesian

political assumptions. Friedman's most central challenge to the prevailing orthodoxy has little to do with the technicalities of monetary policy. It is on whether it is possible to achieve a target level of full employment by manipulating total spending – whether through the budget, monetary policy, the exchange rate or import controls. Friedman returns to an earlier tradition in insisting that the minimum sustainable level of unemployment – the so-called 'natural rate' – is determined by underlying economic forces such as the speed of industrial change, training and mobility, union and other monopolistic restrictions, and a host of other influences. Any attempt to run the economy persistently below the sustainable level will need to be supported by an ever-increasing rate of monetary expansion and the end result will be not merely inflation, but accelerating inflation.

The Friedmanites have not simply gone back to the old orthodoxy. They fully accept that a Keynesian boost to demand can reduce unemployment below the sustainable level for a temporary period. 'Temporary' might have been a decade or even more in the 1950s, when people still thought that a pound was a pound and a dollar was a dollar. Today, when 'money illusion' has practically gone and people bargain in real terms, a 'temporary' boost will, with good fortune, last for two or three years at most.

It is this temporary success, but ultimate futility, of so-called 'Keynesian' spending boosts that is such a trap for a democracy. Not only do such episodes bring no lasting benefit to employment; on the contrary, unemployment will subsequently have to be abnormally high if governments wish to reverse the ensuing inflation, or perhaps just prevent it accelerating. (For a fuller explanation, see my *Second Thoughts on Full Employment Policy*.)

Although it would be absurd to press the question 'On whose side would Keynes have been?', the idea of a sustainable level of unemployment, which could not be reduced further by 'a boost from the centre', occurs several times in Keynes's own papers. He put this level at 800,000 (references are given in *Second Thoughts*) for the pre-war period, when the total labour force was much smaller and social-security benefits were far more restricted than now. Post-war economic models geared exclusively to real output and employment, in which wages and prices depend entirely on the mood of the unions and incomes policy, and in which any increase in the money supply is treated as a minor by-product, seem to me foreign to the spirit of anyone as obsessively interested in money and financial flows as Keynes was.

The difficulties that the 'natural rate' doctrine pose for Keynes's approach are political and not only of economic theory. It is not difficult to think of rules which would prevent unnecessary fluctuations of unemployment above its natural rate, without spending ourselves into 'runaway inflation'.

To understand the political threat posed by short-term temptations of money creation and excessive deficit spending, it is helpful to turn to the analysis of democracy of one of Keynes's contemporaries, the Austrian–American economist Joseph Schumpeter (see his *Capitalism, Socialism and Democracy*). One is not surprised to find that the two thinkers had very little understanding of each other.

Schumpeter's analysis starts with the truism that democracy in a large country cannot be – as the literal-minded see it – the rule of all the people by all the people. There are, at least for the foreseeable future, limits to the ability of technological progress in communications which make continual consultation of all the people all the time impossible. Even if it were possible, most people might well prefer a less inconvenient and burdensome system of organisation. In any case, there would be the difficulty of weighting the importance of different views on issues where people's interests, knowledge and feelings are involved to very different degrees.

A more realistic definition of democracy, which would include the essential characteristics of many of the systems of government in the Western hemisphere, was provided by Schumpeter. He conceived of democratic representatives as akin to other economic agents: they deal in votes as steelmen deal in steel or oilmen in oil. The democratic character of their behaviour results from the competition between different politicians and parties for votes. To gain or to regain power, they must offer policies or, more characteristically, promise results that will attract votes away from other potential governments. To this extent, the views of at least part of the electorate will influence the way in which the country is governed.

The electors are assumed to act according to their own self-interest. This does not imply any view of their motives; as individuals, or within small groups, people can display great generosity. In larger groups, however, any individual who does not look after his own interests is likely to suffer in comparison with those who do. It seems realistic, therefore, to assume that voters will, at least at the margin, vote according to their perceived interests.

The commercial market place is characterised by the *individual* pursuit of self-interest. This is unlikely to cause irresistible demands for more than the economy can provide. Individuals in their own lives are subject to budget constraints; they cannot spend more than they can earn or borrow.

The political market place is characterised by the pursuit of self-interest by large groups, where these personal budget constraints are absent. Electors can rather more easily demand an increased slice of the cake without any agreement on the part of those who are supposed to have the thinner slices. The costs of the handouts, whether met through taxation or inflation, will not necessarily accrue to the groups who benefit from them. In each individual case, whether a subsidy is paid to council-house dwellers, cheese eaters or car makers, there is a strong incentive for the interest group to press its demands as forcefully as possible without any real discipline on the sum total of interest-group demands.

Even with fixed rules on public finance, the process will induce a bias toward public expenditure. Nevertheless, because taxpayers or borrowers have votes, an increase in public expenditure which requires an increase in taxation or high interest rates is likely to be somewhat less attractive to a government than an increase which can be financed effectively by printing money. With traditional rules such as the balanced-budget principle, or gold-standard limits on money creation, the bias towards government overspending is likely to have some limits on it by opposition from taxpayers.

If, on the other hand, the government is permitted to boost aggregate demand by extra expenditure without extra taxes or higher interest rates, its trade-off is different. One alternative is to lose votes by failing to offer an interest group as much as other parties offer. The other is to join the competitive bidding and offer as much.

If the effects of printing money on inflation were immediate, the government might have some qualms about substituting, say, temporary, job-preservation for stable prices. But, as the inflationary effects are delayed, the government is presented with a choice between a certain benefit in increased electoral support in the short run and the uncertain cost of some very unpleasant choices between a slump and runaway inflation in some years' time. It is not surprising that governments, conscious of Keynes's view of long-run mortality, accept the inflationary alternative.

In short, therefore, there are two reasons why governments are liable to overstimulate demand, or attempt to promote unsustainably high employment: the benefits are short-run, while the costs are long-run; and the benefits are specific and easily attributable to the government, while the costs are general and less easily attributed to any single cause.

Schumpeter himself was less of a Cassandra than a present-day adherent of his analysis would tend to be. He put forward three main preconditions for the insulation of liberal representative democracy against the internally generated economic forces that would tend to destroy it. It is interesting that these conditions were also part of Keynes's implicit view of the political world. But, because of the latter's underlying optimism about the political process, he did not bother to spell them out himself or consider the circumstances in which they might be endangered.

Schumpeter's three conditions were the limitation of the area of effectively political decision-making, the existence of a well-trained bureaucracy and the exercise of political self-restraint. If these were fulfilled, there would be a greater chance of achieving a Keynesian ideal of a policy in which rational ideas and rational men held sway. It is under these conditions that one could realistically assert, as Keynes did, in the most widely quoted single passage of his *General Theory* (p. 387) that 'The power of vested interests is vastly exaggerated compared with the gradual encroachment of ideas.'

Government by rational men and rational ideas is possible, if at all, only if there are limits to the incursions of vote-seeking politicians. In the UK there have existed a number of special agencies whose non-political nature has been constantly stressed both by themselves and by the government of the day. The pre-1914 Bank of England was a leading example. Keynes may well have envisaged an entire government operation in this fashion. However obscurantist those running such an institution might be, mortality and the permeation of ideas could be relied upon to disseminate enlightened thinking after, at worst, a lag of a generation. Economic debate in such a society would be confined largely to the technical problem of how to manage demand optimally to face existing and expected states of nature, with no danger that demand management would become the tool of competing political teams.

Thus Keynes almost certainly believed that the second Schumpeterian condition, the need for a powerful well-entrenched bureaucracy, was also fulfilled and could keep government in the hands of 'experts'. A government that could, for reasons of prestige or dogma, choose to go back to the pre-1914 gold parity in 1925 at the expense of considerable unemployment would surely be able to resist popular pressures when it was pursuing better ideas which would really promote the public interest.

Besides the evidence that governments could resist democratic pressure if the experts thought it necessary, the theory of government by experts was reinforced in Keynes's era by the class composition and attitudes of politicians and civil servants. Politicians of all main parties were, to some extent, enlightened amateurs with sufficient means and independence to resist democratic pressures, while many bureaucrats were for similar reasons able to resist the pressure of politicians. Neither group was under financial pressure to continue at their posts carrying out tasks in which they no longer believed. There was a division of labour between the politicians, who were professionals at dealing in votes, and the bureaucrats, who were professionals at policy analysis. Since economic policy-making clearly fell into the domain of the second group, demand management could be insulated from political pressures.

The existence of a large sector of government that could be insulated to some extent from democratic pressures was both made possible and further reinforced by Schumpeter's third condition for the success of democracy: the existence of tolerance and democratic self-control. In the UK in the earlier part of the twentieth century, electorates were able to exercise this self-restraint partly because they were slow to realise their power, and partly because of a series of *ad hoc* events, such as the First World War, which produced an external threat and a patriotic myth to override sectional conflicts or the Great Depression, which weakened the pressure which could be exerted by unions on industry and government alike.

But just as important was an ethic, which took a long time to erode, which limited the demands on the sharing-out functions of the state. Personal success was seen by nineteenth-century defenders of capitalism as having a firm connection with duty performed. In a society permeated by a Puritan ethic it was agreed that there was a strong correlation between certain personal virtues – frugality, industry, sobriety, reliability, piety – and the way in which power, privilege and property were distributed.

This partly spurious correlation was mistakenly taken to be the sign of a just – not merely a free – society. The public morality of capitalist bourgeois society was, however, inevitably a transitional one. On its own grounds it could not hope to stand up to serious analysis. Luck was always as important as merit in the gaining of awards; and merit is inherently a subjective concept in the eye of the beholder. Society was living on the moral heritage of the feudal system. A mediaeval king was expected to 'do justice and to render each his due'. It was not a matter of what the king thought a subject ought to have, or what the subject thought best for himself, but what belonged to him according to custom, which in turn was supported by theological sanctions.

For a long time capitalist civilisation was able to live on this feudal legacy, and the aura of legitimacy was transferred from the feudal lord to the employer, from the mediaeval hieararchy of position to that derived from the luck of the market place. But this feudal legacy was bound to be extinguished by the torchlight of secular and rationalistic inquiry, which was itself so closely associated with the rise of capitalism. The personal qualities of middle-class leaders did not help to kindle that affection for the social order which is probably necessary if it is not to be blamed for the inevitable tribulations and disappointments of most people's lives. Modern politicians and business chiefs lack the glamour of an aristocracy. With neither the trappings of tradition nor the heroic qualities of great war leaders or generals, they cannot excite the identification or hero worship which previously reconciled people to much greater differences of wealth and position than exist today.

But without the self-restraint of the electorate, the other two preconditions for the successful combination of democracy with demand management – the limitation of political decision, and the key role of the mandarin class – have inevitably crumbled. The area of effective political decision-making has been vastly enlarged from its size in the inter-war period, while the independence of the bureaucracy from political pressure has declined. Moreover, in so far as the bureaucracy has been able to promote its own interests, it has itself come to operate in the same direction as other interest groups rather than as an élite which does not have to lobby for jobs and privilege. It thus tends to stimulate rather than discourage the excessive expectations of the electorate. The public sector has itself become an important lobby for increased public expenditure.

Keynes died in 1946 and we do not have the benefit of his observations on the new social and political environment (which could hardly have failed to distress him aesthetically, whatever his final judgment). Unfortunately, a system of economic thinking was developed in his name which rationalised the most self-destructive tendencies of democracy, instead of acting as a bulwark against them. To escape from our predicament we need not another revolution in economic theory, but a revolution in constitutional and political ideas which will save us from the snare of unlimited democracy, before we find ourselves with no democracy – and very little freedom – left. The widespread call for 'a new Keynes' reflects the worst aspect the great man's legacy: the belief that we can make deep-seated problems go away by a few tactical gimmicks which can be applied costlessly by a few clever men in an office.

7 Inflation as an Industrial Problem

AUBREY JONES

J. M. Keynes appeared in several guises. Two only are of relevance to this discussion: the Keynes of post-1918 and the Keynes of the mid-1930s. The first was concerned with the conquest of inflation; the second with the conquest of unemployment.

Common to all guises there was, however, a single trait. Keynes had imbibed economics from Marshall, who in his day had come to economics through ethics. Marshall saw in economics a means for the alleviation of poverty. Keynes's preoccupation likewise was with the improvement of the human lot. This view of economics differed from that which I was taught at the London School of Economics; at my alma mater, if my fading memory does not fail me, it was professed that economics was ethically neutral and was concerned only with the 'efficient' allocation of scarce resources. Subsequent observation of life has led me to believe that this was too narrow an approach, though even as undergraduate I could not fully grasp how one and the same mind could divide itself into two parts – one, that of the economists, which was ethically neutral, and one, that of the citizen, which was bound to have some ethical view of human, and therefore economic, relationships.

Be that as it may, the point of immediate importance is that a solution to the economic problems of the post-Keynes world – if there be one – requires more than a narrowly economic approach; it needs the help of other social sciences; and policy-making today suffers from the disposition of economics to hug itself unto itself and insist on its purity as an academic discipline. This, it will be seen, is something which Keynes foresaw.

But to begin with the Keynes of 1918. With the end of the

50

First World War there was a quick return to what were thought to be the halcyon days of *laissez-faire*. All controls (including rationing) were hurled on the bonfire; and the vast volume of purchasing power pent up during the war was suddenly unleashed upon the free market. The consequent inflation caused Keynes to fear for the survival of the capitalist system itself, for how could savers lend and producers borrow without some assurance about future prices? In this giddy atmosphere of freedom, with the joint stock banks enjoying a high degree of independence, Keynes advocated a steep increase in the rate of interest and a policy of dear money designed to break businessmen's expectations. It was all he could do given the prevailing traditions, though in retrospect he feared that even his own remedy, had it been acted upon, would not have been enough and that a greater degree of interventionism by the Bank of England would have been appropriate.

By the mid-1930s Keynes had moved on. Already, by the mid-1920s, after the restoration of the pound sterling to its pre-1914 parity with other currencies, he had foreseen serious consequences 'if we continue to apply the principles of an economics which was worked out on the hypothesis of *laissez-faire* and free competition, to a society which is rapidly abandoning these hypotheses'. Ten years later he had developed an answer to the inter-war problem of persistent unemployment. It did not lie in a downward pressure on wages (as advocated by Pigou in his *Theory of Unemployment*), partly because, on practical grounds, it was not easy to see how wages could in fact be pushed down, and partly because, even on theoretical grounds, a contraction in wages would contract demand and so fail to give businessmen the incentive to expand. The answer lay rather in an act of intervention by the government – the use, that is, by government of its annual budget to balance, not so much its own expenditure and revenues, but rather supply and demand in the economy as a whole. This thought implied that, when there was heavy unemployment and insufficient private demand to absorb it, the government should deliberately create demand by incurring a budgetary deficit.

As a result, since the early 1940s, in Britain at any rate, budgets have aimed at the larger objective of national economic balance rather than at the lesser objective of balance in the government's housekeeping accounts. Not that the balance has always been achieved. Sometimes demand has been in excess of supply and there has been, as some would put it, 'over-employment'. At other times supply has been in excess of demand, and employment has been reduced. Nearly always the attempts at balance have overshot the mark. Even so, since the Second World War, countries have enjoyed a consistently faster rate of economic growth and less marked fluctuations than in the inter-war years and possibly than at any other time in history. This was the legacy which Keynes bequeathed.

The boon carried with it, however, a penalty: inflation, accelerating by and large with the passage of the years. Keynes foresaw the problem. He realised that, as full employment was approached, demand would press on supply, and wages, and with them prices, would tend to rise. What would he today have done about it? Clearly one can only speculate.

Would he, as in 1920, have advocated a policy of dear money? It is doubtful, for in 1920 he saw the excess of purchasing power over capacity as so enormous that it could be safely reduced without causing much unemployment. Further, he recognised that monetary policy might have an effect on wages only in so far as it increased unemployment; it could thus operate only indirectly. According to Professor Moggridge's recent book on Keynes, monetary policy was therefore seen as 'singularly ill adapted' to achieving a reduction in incomes. As somebody familiar with the City he would also have known that there were limits to which a monetary policy could be pushed: applied too tightly it could provoke bankruptcies and these in their turn could undermine confidence in the banking system itself; why else the recent 'lifeboat' operations of the big banks to rescue the banks on the fringe? And he would probably have concurred with a view recently expressed by Arthur Burns, chairman of the US Federal Reserve Board: 'You know, all this talk about the growth of money misses the point that what is important about money, particularly in the short run, is the willingness to use it – not the size of the stock or the rate at which the stock is growing.'

More fundamentally, Keynes did not recognise the wages

problem as monetary or economic; he saw it as 'political'. Three quotations, taken from Professor Moggridge's book, will suffice. All three are extracts from letters written between December 1944 and June 1945. 'I do not doubt that a serious problem will arise when we have a combination of collective bargaining and full employment. But I am not sure how much light the analytical [economic] method you apply can throw on this essentially political problem.' 'The task of keeping efficiency-wages reasonably stable ... is a political rather than an economic problem.' And finally, in a comment on the Australian White Paper on Full Employment, 'One is also, simply because one knows no solution, inclined to turn a blind eye to the wages problem in a full employment economy.'

Thus Keynes, having solved one problem himself, left us with another to solve ourselves, hinting that to do so we must move outside the field of economics into the 'political'. What could he conceivably have meant by the word 'political'?

Despite a temptation to idealise what has been lost, there is a fair unanimity of view that before industrialisation the craftsman was a creator, in the sense that he had reasonable discretion as to how to shape his work. In addition there was at least a tacit, if not an acknowledged, bond of reciprocal obligation between master and servant, and therefore between man and man. With industrialisation, or with mechanisation, which was the form which industrialisation first took, all this changed. The division of labour – the secret of efficiency – caused the worker to lose the sense of creation and to become more of an automaton, doing routine repetitive work. Meanwhile his superiors retained full discretionary powers, determining in detail what he should do and enforcing strict supervision over the manner in which he did it. Thus, to use Marxian terminology, the worker became 'alienated' from his potential self, and 'alienated' also from his superiors and thus from other men. In these circumstances his only recourse was to form an alliance with others 'alienated' like himself – in other words, to form a trade union.

The fundamental political problem ever since has been twofold: first, how, within an enterprise, to restore between managed and managers the broken bond, to recreate a sense of common interest; secondly, how, within a competitive capitalist system in which man is divided from man, to instil into competing units, be they firms or trade unions, a sense of belonging to a greater whole. At one moment it seemed that the supersession of mechanisation by automation would have solved the problem for one, that at least it would have given the worker a greater sense of creativity. There is no evidence, however, that such has been the case, and attitudes formed over 200 years of industrialisation have tended to harden, with the feeling of 'alienation' spreading ever further up the hierarchical ladder.

There are several possible approaches to the problem. First, there is what one might call the traditional conservative or paternalistic approach. This approach recognises that managers owe the managed an obligation, an obligation which can be fulfilled by various welfare arrangements. The approach is admirable in intent, but in historical terms it is spitting in the face of the wind, and for that reason alone it can, after a long apparent success, provoke a violent reaction against it, as in the case of the strike at Pilkingtons in 1970.

Secondly, there is the Marxist approach. The Marxist would argue that the 'alienated', though reinforced through a trade union, can never achieve parity of bargaining power with the managers; for the managers are identified with the wealthy, the wealthy command the vehicles of communication and propaganda, and the managed therefore are at least half-conditioned to an acceptance of the society which the managers want. This is the intellectual case of the militant, and there is something to it. The trouble lies not with the analysis, but with the answer. For, if all wealth is transferred to the state, the state alone will command all the vehicles of communication, and the conditioning of the managed to an acceptance of the society governed by the managers will be complete. Further, the problem arises from the differentiation of tasks and responsibilities; it thus remains unaffected by a change in ownership. That said, it is possibly true that the bond between managed and managers can be reforged through massive indoctrination.

Thirdly, there is the balance-of-power approach. This approach sees the managed as having attained an equality of bargaining power with the managers, an equality that it welcomed in that power, rather than being concentrated is, as any respectable constitution would have it, divided. This is roughly the position described by the TUC in its evidence in 1966 to the Donovan Commission on Trade Unions and Employers' Associations. According to this approach, there is no reason why this equality should not conduce to stability and the public interest, so long as militants on either side of the balance do not overplay their hand.

Fourthly and lastly, there is the approach of the contemporary Conservatives, or the excessive-power approach. According to this approach, the managed have now attained an advantage in bargaining power over the managers. It is this thinking which lay behind the Industrial Relations Act of 1971, and it has a long history. It was mentioned in the Webbs' book on *Industrial Democracy* in 1902: when 'workmen combine the balance is redressed, and may even incline, as against the isolated employer, in favour of the wage-earner', resulting 'in a strong union relentlessly enforcing its will on the capitalists, without deigning to consult with them beforehand'.

Now, the difference between the third and the fourth approaches – that is, the difference between the approach which presupposes a rough equality of bargaining power between managed and managers, and that which considers that the bargaining power of the managed is superior – is less than the protagonists of either might think. What matters is the bargaining power of the managers as against the consumer. If one assumes, as one must, granted the importance attached to economies of scale, that, to use the terminology of Sir John Hicks, 'fixprice' markets have increasingly displaced 'flexprice' markets, then the bargaining power of the managers against the consumer is considerable. They can pass on the increased labour costs, no matter whether they arise from an equality or an inferiority of bargaining power *vis-à-vis* the managed. And this can happen under conditions of full employment or less than full employment.

We are then faced with a situation described by Alan Fox in a quotation, presumably from the Webbs, in his excellent book *Beyond Contract: Work, Power and Trust Relations,* in which 'the economic conditions of the parties concerned are unequal' and 'legal freedom of contract merely enables the superior in strategic strength to dictate the terms'. In its original context, this quotation may have been intended to relate only to managed against managers, but it relates equally to managers against consumers. It is this situation which is the foundation of the case for government intervention and calls for some kind of political action. But what action? The most one can do here is to outline certain possible organisational arrangements.

The crux of the problem is the passage onwards into a price increase of an increase in labour costs. It would be desirable, therefore, for the full implications for prices of an impending wage settlement or settlements to be expounded to the potential signatories and to the public at large before the settlement is sealed. This exposition cannot be made by the managers, for they would be suspected by the managed of over-pitching the resulting price. Nor can it be made by the managed, for they would be regarded by the managers as under-pitching the price. The exposition can be made without raising suspicion only by an independent organisation. And this organisation would not be dealing in generalities, such as the fact that wage settlements do have an effect on prices. It would be dealing with the effect on prices of selected important wage claims, while, it is to be hoped, there is still time – or time can be ensured – to influence the outcome.

Now, a wage claim seldom applies to all the workers in an enterprise. It normally applies to part only, though this part may be large in relation to the total, as in coalmining, or small, as sometimes in the car industry. Even when the claim emanates from a small proportion of the employees, its settlement has a rippling effect throughout the entire enterprise. The organisation charged with estimating the likely effect on prices would have to take this rippling effect into account.

Its task in doing so would be eased if the enterprise had a job-evaluation scheme in which jobs were ranked in order of importance. There is no reason why it should not be made mandatory on all firms above a certain size to have a job-evaluation scheme. The organisation could act as guide and mentor in the establishment and supervision of such a scheme, which should be jointly determined by managers and managed. Possibly the most important factor in determining the ranking should be discretionary power or responsibility partly because different degrees of responsibility roughly reflect different degrees of skill, partly because a relationship between responsibility and pay has come to be regarded as 'fair'. I should not be averse, however, to showing some bias in favour of those with little power of discretion, just because their work was humdrum. Unions representing employees at different parts in the hierarchy of the enterprise would still negotiate on behalf of their members. But they would be negotiating with a standard of relative importance in work, and therefore relative fairness, in the background. If relative pay fell out of line with relative importance in work, then somewhere there would be manifest injustice. And it is to be noted that in determining relative importance in work industrial democracy would have a part to play.

When a wage claim by a group within a particular enterprise is launched, however, it is not only the rest of the enterprise which is affected: other industries may be affected too. The task of any independent organisation may then become much more difficult. It may be possible for it to compare the importance of a job in one industry with that of a job in another industry, but to develop this technique would take time. Nor would it be the only consideration which would have to be taken into account. Attention would have to be paid to the prospective rise and fall of different industries, and of different rates of movement in output per head in different industries. Nonetheless, it would be an obligation on the organisation to pronounce on the implications for prices of a particular wage claim before the claim is settled. If the implications for specific prices were deemed 'excessive', it would be for the government to call in aid the TUC or CBI or both, and invite them to exercise their influence in abating the potential settlement.

No doubt the arrangements briefly sketched above have their defects. The important point, however, is that they differ fundamentally from the arrangements now in force in the UK. The present arrangements leave largely unchanged relationships in pay between different working groups, in accordance with formulae laid down primarily by the TUC; the relationships therefore are by nature unstable. The resulting wage settlement is then taken as a given fact by the Prices Commission when determining prices. By contrast, the arrangements suggested in this article provide for changes in relationships in pay between different working groups; and the effect on prices should be announced before their happening, not after. Above all, the present arrangements are designed to meet an emergency; the arrangements proposed would attempt to meet the political problem which Keynes saw – that his own cure for unemployment had aggravated the need for new and permanent institutions to bring home to the fragmented parts of industrialised society the effect of their actions on the whole.

8 The Radical Keynes

ROBERT LEKACHMAN

For forty years three versions of Keynesian doctrine have lurked within the covers of *The General Theory of Employment, Interest and Money,* economic gospels of conservative, liberal, and radical temper. According to the initial version, nothing much was wrong with contemporary capitalism that a bit of intelligent tinkering could not cure. Those timid beasts, the businessmen, would expand their investments and set off euphoric multiplier effects upon national income and employment if, but only if, politicians took pains to speak kindly to them, shove interest rates lower, and run the economy at gently inflationary rates. In this mood, Keynes was likely to criticise Franklin Roosevelt for scaring sensitive American corporate types with his loose talk of driving the moneychangers out of the temple and punishing malefactors of great wealth.

When Keynes in Chapter 18 got around to summarising his own analysis, he commenced with this notorious paragraph:

> 'We take as given the existing skill and quantity of available labour, the existing quality and quantity of available equipment the existing technique, the degree of competition, the tastes and habits of the consumer, the disutility of different intensities of labour, and of the activities of supervision and organisation, as well as the social structure including the forces . . . which determine the distribution of the national income.

Although in the very next sentence Keynes insisted that 'This does not mean that we assume these factors to be constant', the context made it plain that 'the degree of competition' which Keynes took for granted approximated Marshallian

59

assumptions of sufficient competition in most markets to guarantee quick responses by sellers to shifts in the demand for their products. Certainly there were few suggestions at any point in the *General Theory* that private monopoly was a force to be reckoned with.

For the most part, however, Keynes's judgment of the efficacy of monetary policy was strongly coloured by his glum perception of the investment outlook, for he feared that in the long run the marginal efficiency of capital, his term for expected profits, must decline. Here, of course, he wrote in the tradition of nineteenth-century classical economics, both Ricardian and Marxian, which forecast, though for contrasting reasons, declining profits. This second gospel was popularised in the United States in the late Alvin Hansen's famous 1938 presidential speech to the American Economic Association as the secular stagnation hypothesis. Investment possibilities were fated to narrow because population growth was slowing, the western frontier remained obstinately closed, and less was to be anticipated from technical innovation in the future than in the past.

Within the *General Theory* Keynes was only an occasional secular stagnationist. Many of his *obiter dicta* held open the possibility that a combination of tax and financial incentives to private business and direct deficit outlays by government might fill the gap between underemployment and full employment. Here and there this advocacy of what came to be called fiscal policy took bravura form, as in his splendid discourses on the economic virtues of Egyptian pyramids, mediaeval cathedrals, buried bottles full of cash and other wasteful expenditures which possessed the merit, all the same, of promoting more sensible spending on the goods and services which filled human needs.

Textbook versions of Keynesian aggregative equilibrium, such as all ten editions of Samuelson and the many volumes which imitate him, now combine monetary and fiscal policy as equally desirable implements of economic management. Although texts published within the last two or three years are influenced by the unsettling experience of stagflation, Samuelson's coinage for an unpleasing simultaneous appearance of inflation and unemployment, respectable expositions of Keynes still preach the optimistic message that reasonably steady economic growth accompanied by acceptable price and employment behaviour is possible if public policy is astute and unions and corporations restrain their avarice.

Here, of course, is the occasion of this essay. Although Keynes did casually admit in the *General Theory* that inflation might be troublesome even before full employment was reached, he ascribed the possibility to the emergence of supply bottlenecks which pushed wages or prices higher and, on occasion, spread to portions of the economy in which unused capacity still persisted. Keynes, at least in the *General Theory*, failed to examine possible concentrations of market power which allowed suppliers of either goods or labour to extract higher prices or wages even at the cost of lost sales or fewer jobs. One of the more striking American phenomena of current experience was the pricing policy of General Motors and its friendly rivals during the 1973–5 mini-depression. During this period, the auto companies sharply marked up their prices even though the customers were fleeing showrooms in hordes and sales plummeted to their lowest levels in two decades.

This is to say that, wherever one, two, or three huge corporations dominate an important industry, that industry can choose between alternative combinations of high prices and small sales, and low prices and larger sales. When the unions are the stronger party, they enjoy similar discretion in the choice of either higher wages and fewer jobs, or lower wages and more jobs. The market for services is by no means exempt from seller dominion over both sides of the supply–demand equation. In the United States once more, lawyers, at least until the Supreme Court rebuked the practice (as it did recently), circulated minimum fee schedules to protect their members from price competition. Tidy coalitions of physicians, hospitals, health insurers and amiable federal regulators have pushed the cost of American medical care upwards at a pace double that of inflation in general.

Ever since A. W. Phillips published his famous article, it has been fashionable to assert the presence of a trade-off between inflation and unemployment. As the tale is often told, during spells of high employment labour discipline falters, absenteeism and other varieties of bloody-mindedness flourish, unions press wage claims far beyond the frontiers of imaginable productivity improvement, employers, kicking and groaning, pass their higher costs onward to customers (usually with a profit sweetener to ease the pain), higher prices become the sufficient reason for still larger wage claims, and so on, until in self-defence some Iron Chancellor slams on the fiscal and monetary brakes.

The Phillips hypothesis assumes stability of profit and wage shares and a sturdy tendency of employers and unions to react against any erosion of their shares. It implies also, as did Keynes, that both prices and wages are flexible enough to respond quickly to increases or decreases in the demand for products or workers. But, as Britons and Americans can ruefully testify, theory runs counter to current history. In Britain, where many unions are more powerful and more bellicose than their American counterparts, wages until recently rose at dangerously high speed even though unemployment also rose far beyond the symbolic million mark. Because American managers are stronger and their unions weaker, prices until the middle of 1975 rose more rapidly than wages, even though economic activity and employment subsided to figures unprecedented since 1940. The moderate expansion which began early in 1975 and picked up speed in 1976 (a presidential election year), has left unemployment hanging at well over 7 per cent, itself a figure plausibly attacked by trade-union economists as an underestimate by at least 2 or 3 percentage points.

Among American economists of conservative or even moderate views, the new fashion is to argue that 6 or 7 per cent unemployment is tolerable because so many of the unemployed are mere women, untrained and under-educated blacks, and restless teenagers – groups, it is implied, which suffer less because of their jobless condition than do male, white heads of households. Certainly by the criteria of such influential Keynesians of the Kennedy–Johnson era as Walter Heller, Gardner Ackley and Arthur Okun, the three chairmen of Democratic Councils of Economic Advisers, such unemployment targets mark a substantial retreat from the 'interim' goal of 4 per cent unemployment enunciated a mere fifteen years ago.

Not particularly aided by their economic advisers,

parliamentary governments swing uneasily between spells of monetary and fiscal austerity which operate only indifferently to curb inflation but certainly do succeed in enlarging unemployment, and, in good time for the next election, renewal of fiscal and monetary stimulation, which customarily speeds up inflation but manages only moderately to reduce unemployment. Such stop–go episodes, as notorious in the United States as in Britain, are especially damaging to economies whose growth is slow, as it has been in both countries since 1945 by comparison with the economic growth of the international league leaders – West Germany and Japan.

Thus it appears that Keynes Mark I and Keynes Mark II are equally irrelevant to this decade's central economic issue, reconciliation within the framework of political democracy and private ownership of much or most of the productive apparatus, of group claims for more of the national product than can be made available. The problem is all the more acute because OPEC has taught the industrialised nations a lesson which other raw material producers are all too eager to emulate: resources are both finite and susceptible to political manipulation.

When growth slows or stops entirely, one group can gain only at the expense of another. As Rudolf Klein has put the point, 'Immediately the competition for resources becomes a zero-sum game. One man's prize is another man's loss. If the blacks want to improve their share of desirable goods, it can only be at the expense of whites. If the over-sixty-fives are to be given higher pensions, or improved services, it can only be at the expense of the working population or the young.' In such communities, fears Klein, 'It would seem only too likely that the haves would man the barricades to defend their share of resources against the have-nots. The politics of compromise would be replaced by the politics of revolution, because the have-nots would be forced to challenge the whole basis of society, and its distribution of wealth and power.'

Whether or not shifts in income distribution justify such extreme pessimism, whether, as Robert Heilbroner fears, democracy is itself doomed in the longer run because quarrels over resources within nations and between nations will tear societies apart is, perhaps fortunately, the sort of question to which no firm answer can be given. There is, as might be expected, a more cheerful vision of the future in Keynes, the last of his three perspectives. This is the picture sequestered in the *General Theory's* final chapter, 'Concluding Notes on the Social Philosophy Towards which the General Theory Might Lead'. Economists, no more than other readers, pay much attention to the last pages of difficult books, particularly when they are able to extract delightful mathematical models from the analysis which preceded the mere words of social reflection with which Keynes ended his great intellectual enterprise.

It is interesting and rewarding to reread the fourteen pages of Chapter 24. Keynes began by noting that 'The outstanding faults of the economic society in which we live are its failure to provide full employment and its arbitrary and inequitable distribution of income and wealth.' No considerations of growth and efficiency justified this maldistribution. 'There is', he allowed, 'social and psychological justification for significant inequalities of incomes and wealth, but not such large disparities as exist today.' Inequality was ethically outrageous and dangerous to the hope of full employment, for it limited consumer demand and diminished the incentive to invest.

Thus, if the marginal efficiency of capital was in any case fated to decline, Keynes's preferred policies included income redistribution which enlarged the propensity to consume, and public policy 'directed to increasing and supplementing the inducement to invest'. Keynes, an intense individualist, hoped that much scope would remain for personal choices of all varieties, but his programme specifically contemplated the 'euthanasia of the rentier', the 'vital importance of establishing certain central controls in matters which are now left in the main to individual initiative', and the exercise by the state of a 'guiding influence on the propensity to consume'. Since banking policy by itself was unlikely to 'determine an optimum rate of investment', Keynes was prepared for stronger measures: 'I conceive, therefore, that a somewhat comprehensive socialisation of investment will prove the only means of securing an approximation to full employment; though this need not exclude all manner of compromises and of devices by which public authority will co-operate with private initiative.'

Keynes knew perfectly well what he was saying: 'The central controls necessary to ensure full employment will, of course, involve a large extension of the traditional fucntions of government.' The curious irrelevance to public debate of standard Keynesian analysis is the result of stubborn resistance on the part of conventional economists to the structural features of economies in which the free markets of their models are less and less important and allocation of resources is dominated by the interplay between private market power and government authorities, who sometimes resist that power but more often serve the will of those who wield it.

The societies of the West are engaged in inchoate debate over the goals and techniques of planning. Planning of the French and Japanese variety occurs under the influence and control of major industrial and financial interests. The socialisation of investment which is achieved under such auspices naturally protects property interests and preserves existing disparities of income and wealth. Nevertheless, when such planning is intelligently handled, attention is paid to job protection and adequate levels of social services. On the record, French and Japanese planners have done far less well in the control of inflation. Struggles over income shares continue.

The recent upsurge of interest in economic planning in the United States centres upon a mild measure sponsored by Senators Hubert Humphrey and Jacob Javits. The notion of some sort of planning has attracted the approval of alert business types like Henry Ford II, Felix Rohatyn of Lazard Frères, and W. Michael Blumenthal of Bendix. Ideological confusion on the subject is underscored by the vehement opposition to any variety of planning by Walter Wriston of Citicorp, Thomas Murphy of General Motors, and most of the business press. The rhetoric echoes *The Road to Serfdom*.

It is still another symbol of intellectual confusion that a timid step toward an alternative planning model, closer to the spirit of Keynes, has been sponsored by the same Hubert Humphrey. The Humphrey–Hawkins Full Employment Bill defines 3 per cent unemployment as a goal of national policy to be reached in three years or less, imposes upon the White House and Congress joint responsibility to enact appropriate full-employment programmes, and embodies, despite the pervasive free-enterprise rhetoric, a commitment to direct job creation by the Federal government. Full employment is by itself mildly redistributionist and the tax and other policies needed to achieve it are also likely to diminish inequality.

Keynes implies in Chapter 24 that the hopes of democrats are likeliest to be fulfilled by planning for full employment and redistribution, for it is only within the social context of diminished inequality that social envy diminishes and group claims are tempered. Only in such circumstances are incomes policies at all likely to win general assent and thus attain effective influence upon the rate of inflation. When power determines income shares, the weak will struggle to become stronger and the strong will, as Rudolf Klein said, defend their privileges on the barricades.

It would be reassuring to think that economists will play a part in the movement toward enlightening debate and satisfactory planning. With or without their help, important choices will be made, much as Adolf Hitler and Franklin Roosevelt pursued Keynesian measures several years before Keynes couched them in suitably theoretical form. Those who live by the sword tend to perish by the same sharp implement. Economists who now live by econometric models of vanishing market economies may well die professionally, if not personally, because of their misplaced affections.

I end on a note of tempered optimism. It is unlikely that any advanced economy will successfully yoke together full employment, price stability and steady growth without substantial alterations of existing institutional arrangements and distributions of income, wealth and market power. It is possible, though not highly probable, that the inevitable drift toward planning will be in the wholesome direction of full employment and economic equity Should the future be this pleasant, Chapter 24 of the *General Theory* will become a sacred text and Keynes's hope that economists will become citizens as useful as dentists will at length become reality.

9 Keynes and the Socialists

STUART HOLLAND

Keynes was not a socialist, and was almost wholly ignorant of the work of the founding father of modern socialism – Marx. Yet he had more influence on post-war British socialists than any other theorist of our time. It also is arguable that, almost single-handed, he buried Marxism for a generation of the mainstream British Left.

There were various reasons. For one thing, if not a socialist, Keynes was a profound and effective critic of unregulated capitalism. In *The End of Laisser Faire* (1924) he wrote that 'capitalism in itself is in many ways objectionable', and meant it. The acceptance of unemployment to regulate wages and prices offended him through its implied waste of skill and its offence to human dignity. He was no friend of the profit motive. He attacked the alleged virtues of abstinence and thrift, whereby inequalities in wealth and income had traditionally been justified. He exposed contradictions of a stock market based on short-term speculation and divorced from the long-term investment on which profits themsleves depended.

But, more profoundly, Keynes developed the most powerful theory to date for state intervention to offset depression and unemployment in a capitalist system. His theory that the state should concern itself with the level of expenditure and demand to offset under-consumption – however technical its detail – appealed to commonsense outside the bastions of capitalist orthodoxy.

Yet, at the same time, his emphasis on public demand management challenged the socialist orthodoxy that only public ownership and control of supply could avoid periodic unemployment and waste of resources. By attacking Say's 'law' that – in the long run – demand would always equal supply, Keynes shifted the debate on state intervention from the supply to the demand side of the economy. Combined with recommendations for taxation to reduce major inequalities in wealth and income, the 'new economics' seemed to offer a middle way between over-centralised Soviet planning and an anarchic unplanned capitalist market.

Besides, while rejecting the description of 'socialist', Keynes wrote of his policies as 'socialisation'. As he put it in the *General Theory* (1936), he conceived that 'a somewhat comprehensive socialisation of investment will prove the only means of securing an approximation to full employment. . . . Moreover, the necessary measures of socialisation can be introduced gradually and without a break in the general traditions of society.'

However, such socialisation was mainly supposed to include public expenditure on utilities and public works rather than public enterprise. The private sector also should be assisted by the state, through a range of subsidies and incentives. 'But beyond this no obvious case is made out for a system of state socialism which would embrace most of the economic life of the community. It is not the ownership of the means of production which it is important for the State to assume. If the State is able to determine the aggregate amount of resources devoted to augmenting the instruments and basic reward to those who own them, it will have accomplished all that is necessary.'

Put more simply, the state should socialise demand and expenditure rather than supply and ownership. Through changing tax rates, interest rates and exchange rates, it should influence the level of national and international demand rather than command the heights of production, distribution and exchange. At the level of the firm and industry, it should assure that demand management called forth a flow of goods and services at full employment, where necessary subsidising profits under private ownership, rather than socialising ownership itself.

The 'new economics' of public expenditure and demand management was not entirely new. Much of the analytical framework in which Keynes expressed it was either borrowed from others (notably Kahn and Kalecki) or already formulated and applied in government by the new generation of

Swedish economists. It had a direct intellectual impact, granted the extent to which fatalistic Marxism heralded both a final crisis of capitalism (certainly not incredible in the early 1930s) and underestimated the power of the modern capitalist state to intervene with major public expenditure and demand promotion. The crisis of the early 1930s was seen primarily as a crisis of under-consumption, and Keynes appeared – to some – to have squared the circle of solving the crisis without wholly transforming capitalism.

Keynes's real influence on the British Left in the pre-war period was, however, very limited. Lloyd George and Mosley were two of the most ardent advocates of his economics, but one was outside the Labour Party, and the other left it some years before Keynes published his main work. In the dark days for Labour in 1931, after Macdonald had become the leader of a coalition government, Keynes hoped for a while that he could draft a programme for the Labour Party. He saw much of Kingsley Martin at this time, and hoped that the *New Statesman* might become the vehicle for a policy based on his views. But, for various reasons, the Labour Party leadership was not very interested.

For one thing, the right-wing orthodoxies of the 1929 Labour government, followed by the 'sell-out' of coalition, had thrown Labour back on first principles. However progressive Keynes's arguments might be, they still looked very much like a programme for the better management of capitalism rather than for its transformation. State management of demand could not form a rallying point for the party: public ownership and Clause IV could.

Besides, the Marxist current that had been present in Labour Party thinking since the formation of the Independent Labour Party had never run dry. The crisis of Western capitalism following the 1929 crash and the Depression brought it virtually to flood tide in the course of the 1930s. A number of socialist thinkers stood aside from the new Marxist ferment, notably Hugh Dalton, Douglas Jay and E. F. M. Durbin; but, in general, Marx, not Keynes, became the dominant intellectual power in the mainstream Labour movement.

Not least, the Webbs themselves, who had begun by developing a non-Marxist analysis, came in the 1930s to endorse not only key elements of Marxism but also the Stalinist state socialism of the Soviet Union. This latter commitment, embodied in their *Soviet Communism: a New Civilisation?* (1936) may have been inept (during forced collectivisation and two years before the purges), but it undermined coherent Fabian opposition to both Marxism and extensive socialisation of the means of production.

G. D. H. Cole, who, after the war, was to become an orthodox Keynesian social democrat, nonetheless was a leading exponent of a popularised Marxism in the 1930s. His *What Marx Really Meant* was never uncritical. In particular, he tried to play down Marx's exposition of the labour theory of value, and with it the basis of Marx's theory of exploitation in capitalist society. As a result, it is arguable that he never fulfilled the ambition of his own title. But the book and its influence were significant. Certainly, he did not choose to write a popular volume on '*What Keynes Really Means*'.

Otherwise, Gollancz, Laski and Strachey, the triumvirate of the Left Book Club, with its sensationally large sales even by contemporary paperback standards, committed that series to a wide number of publications whose coherent term of reference was Marx rather than Keynes. Gollancz himself was mainly concerned with the struggle against fascism in continental Europe, where gradual reformism was clearly ineffective. Harold Laski became the dominant exponent of Marxist politics and theory of the state, reaching a far wider audience than the LSE through his *State in Theory and Practice*. He also had a wide-ranging command of continental European Marxism of a kind totally foreign to Keynes, and used it to effect during a decade in which liberal theories of the state were thrown into crisis by events on the continent.

Keynes's insularity – both geographical and intellectual – counted against him in this climate. In a famous letter of 1935 to George Bernard Shaw, who had been pressing him to read Marx, he wrote 'I've made another shot at old K.M. last week, reading the Marx–Engels correspondence just published. I prefer Engels of the two. I can see that they invented a certain method of carrying on and a vile manner of writing, both of which their successors have maintained with fidelity. But if you tell me that they discovered a clue to the economic riddle, still I am beaten – I can discover nothing but out of date controversialising.'

In fact, Keynes saw that Marx had realised the problem of insufficient demand to be a main factor in capitalist crisis through under-consumption, and gives him credit for as much in the *General Theory*. But the credit is in an aside, in company with a plus awarded to Silvio Gesell (to whom Keynes paid much more attention) and Major Douglas. Besides, he referred to the arena of all three writers as an 'underworld'. The real world for Keynes was not that of the struggle for power affecting millions across the Channel – between communism, socialism, liberalism and fascism – but the struggle around King's, Cambridge between the economic theories of Marshall, Edgeworth and Pigou.

It was John Strachey who did most in the 1930s to show Keynes's neglect of the wider terms of reference of contemporary socialist debate. In one sense the two men were equal, by virtue of the intellectual self-confidence that followed from their origin in the English upper middle class. Strachey was not a professional economist, but in a series of books – most notably *The Coming Struggle for Power* (1933), *The Nature of the Capitalist Crisis* (1935) and *The Theory and Practice of Socialism* (1936) – he wrote in a manner neither vile nor unpersuasive which carried on the Marxist tradition in the heartland of the British left.

Put simply, Strachey had read Marx extensively, while Keynes had not. This enabled him to show the extent to which Keynes had grasped only one feature of capitalist crisis – under-consumption. He showed that in Marx's analysis crisis was not simply a matter of too few profits through too little demand, but also embedded in the supply structure of the system. This included both a tendency over the long term to rising capital intensity in production, giving rise to structural unemployment, and a basic disproportion between different sectors and regions of a capitalist economy – factors which were highly relevant to Britain between the wars, granted the relative decline of basic industries such as ship-building, textiles and coal, and which remain relevant today with the net decline in manufacturing employment as a whole.

As importantly, Strachey grasped the extent to which Keynes missed the wood for the trees in thinking that he had transcended both Ricardo and Marx by rejecting the labour theory of value and distribution. Keynes certainly asked why profits were lowered in a depression, but saw the question of where they came from as irrelevant. He castigated those who thought that profitability would be restored provided un-employment lowered wages sufficently, but he hardly questioned the justification for profits in the first place. He stayed entrenched in the neo-classical theory of exchange value, determined by supply and demand.

Such a theory of value, as Strachey stressed right into the 1950s (*Contemporary Capitalism*, 1956) has a clear commonsense appeal. The value of goods and services is determined on the market, by prices in exchange. It is a broad path down which most professional economists have strolled and played – often with themselves – for years. But in terms of key issues it is a cul-de-sac, leading nowhere. By contrast, the labour theory of value is an unmade road, but it leads to the heart of the problem of economic justice, social class and equality. It sees profits not as a reward for forgone consumption, but as a con-sequence of the power of capitalists to command labour power, and pay labour less than the full value of its produc-tion.

The impact of this wider-ranging Marxist analysis through the broad Left in the 1930s found its reflection in the National Executive of the Labour Party and its new leader, Clement Attlee. It is not by accident that Anthony Crosland was to claim as much in the first chapter of his anti-Marxist *Future of Socialism* in 1956, drawing specific reference to Attlee's *The Labour Party in Perspective* (1937). As Attlee wrote there, 'the ex-istence of wide disparities of wealth, with a consequent segregation of the community into separate classes, is inimical to true social life. To abolish classes is not so chimerical an un-dertaking as it would have appeared some years ago. . . . The aim of the Socialist State must be equality. This must be the guiding principle applied in its plans of organisation.'

Yet Keynes still became the dominant intellectual influence for a quarter of a century on the post-war British Labour Par-ty. How did it happen?

For one thing, the *General Theory*, his major statement, did not appear until 1936. It made a greater impact on academic economists in the later 1930s and during the war than had the host of articles, pamphlets and other writings that Keynes had published hitherto. A generation of new Labour intellectuals, mainly from Oxbridge, found themselves not only on Labour benches in the parliament of 1945, but also profoundly under Keynes's influence. Not least, public expenditure, partly via the welfare state, sustained more-buoyant levels of employment in post-war Britain than had hitherto been imaginable. Progressive taxation appeared to squeeze the rich, and was seen as a viable instrument for the abolition of major class differences. In short, under-consumption may have been only one of the factors in capitalist crisis, but in the 1930s it had been the dominant one, and Keynesianism seemed to have licked it.

Added to this, not all of the young-generation Marxists in the 1930s were as careful students of Marx as were Strachey, Laski and other key leaders of Left opinion. Many had been seduced by the emotional appeal of Marxism (and in some cases communism), had followed the Webbs in uncritical support of state planning in the Soviet Union, and had seen Stalin as Europe's only hope against Hitler, Mussolini and Franco. The purges in Russia in the late 1930s, the failure of Stalin to support broad-Left popular-front policies in Spain, and the Nazi-Soviet pact led to a disillusion deeper than the previous commitment. Having deified the Soviets, many found that Stalin had failed them, and thereby sought to reject also the old-testament prophet of communism, Marx. The Cold War and its warriors in the late 1940s and early 1950s found their seed falling on fertile ground in the Labour Party.

Also, capitalism in Western Europe and Japan was achieving super-growth of a kind which had rarely been equalled in the Soviet Union, and this in societies which clearly were freer than the so-called democratic socialist republics. It did not much matter that Keynesian policies had little to do with such economic miracles, nor that they depended on conditions of massive labour reserves (Japan, Germany and Italy) or direct state intervention in production planning (France, Japan and Italy). Both in economic and political terms, capitalism not only had survived the war but had recovered in a manner unanticipated by fatalistic Marxism.

Further, direct state intervention through ownership and control, as introduced through the Nationalisation Acts of the 1945-51 Labour governments, had not delivered the brave new world which many had expected. There was relatively little grasp of the fact that the nationalisations actually undertaken were in basic industries and utilities which governments of Left, Right and Centre elsewhere in Western Europe had been undertaking as essential infrastructure for profitable private manufacturing and services.

To a substantial extent the 1945 Labour programme for nationalisation was founded on industry policies still based on the programme of 1918. Over the intervening years the 'commanding heights' of the economy had advanced to new products, processes and techniques beyond the basic-industries sector. If the achievements of the post-war Labour governments in extending public ownership had been considerable, and seen by many in the party as only a first step to further socialisation, Keynes's case on public expenditure and demand management rather than public enterprise was reinforced by the extent to which the welfare state and relatively full employment appeared to have transformed British capitalism.

This argument was notably forwarded by Anthony Crosland in his *Future of Socialism* (1956). Crosland argued that 'Marx has little or nothing to offer the contemporary socialist, either in respect of practical policy, or of the correct analysis of our society, or even of the right conceptual tools or framework.' Drawing attention to the achievements of progressive taxation and welfare expenditure, the major reduction of unemployment, the extension of basic nationalisation, and the political freedom of British society, Crosland questioned whether Britain was still capitalist. He saw conservatism rather than capitalism as the fundamental problem (*The Conservative Enemy*, 1962). He was in favour of planning, provided that it remained general and for the most part indirect, concerned with the extension of public expenditure rather than public enterprise. And he saw Labour ministers capable of undertaking such planning in office, exercising state power in the public interest. Crosland articulated a Keynesian case for economic management and social progress. Though, like Keynes, he never drafted an economic programme for the Labour Party, he represented the progressive Keynesian social democracy which was to dominate Labour thinking in the approach to the 1964 general election, and the Labour governments up to 1970.

In government in the 1960s, such optimism in the power of Labour to manage the economy through indirect intervention suffered a severe setback. The National Plan of 1965, based substantially on Keynesian growth theory and expenditure, was first swamped by the biggest balance-of-payments deficit since the war, then suffocated shortly after its first birthday by the deflationary package of July 1966. Keynesians in the Cabinet argued that the abandonment of the National Plan, with the failure of the increased growth from which major public expenditure was to be financed, reflected an unreadiness to follow Keynes's own prescription of an 'appropriate' devaluation early enough in the lifetime of the government. Few ministers argued that only new public enterprise could assure the expansion from which new social expenditure could be financed. Steel was renationalised as a token to Clause IV orthodoxies, which it was assumed were dying, if not dead. Keynes still seemed to have buried Marx in mainstream Labour thinking.

But in practice new currents, based partly on Marxist analysis and partly on appreciation of the limited role of Keynesianism, were emerging in the Labour movement during the 1960s, and surfaced as a new challenge in the Labour party in the period 1970–4.

For one thing, a generation either unconceived or in infancy in the period of the post-war Labour governments had discovered a hitherto unpublished 'early Marx' – more humanist and less determinist than some of the economic works of Marx in his maturity. The sociological emphasis on alienation in Marx's early writings gave a new base for analysis of the suppression of individualism and self-expression in the economistic values of capitalist society. The limits of state power to transform capitalism by gradual rather than fundamental reforms gained strength not only from the practical failure of Labour between 1964 and 1970, but also from increased attention to Marxist analysis of the modern capitalist state, and realisation that international pressures would resist rising public expenditure as a means of humanising capitalism.

Besides, elements in Marx's analysis of the trend to monopoly power, argued in the 1950s by Baran and Sweezy and, in Britain, by Strachey were bringing the question of public ownership of the means of production back to the forefront of mainstream Labour thinking. The very dynamism of the 'long boom' of post-war capitalism had seen an unprecedented increase in the power of big business. In Britain, in the key manufacturing sector left in private hands by the post-war nationalisations, the top 100 companies had increased their market share from a fifth to a half of the market. In direct exports – so notoriously subject to deficit in the 1960s and 1970s, seventy-five firms had come to command half the trade. In addition, foreign capital investment had reached astronomic totals, with a value of production by British business abroad equal to more than double total direct exports, and five times the foreign production (relative to exports) of key competitors such as Germany or Japan.

In other words, the issues of the structure of supply rather than demand, of chronic disporportion and of direct rather than indirect Keynesian controls had been brought to the forefront of debate by both analysis and events. Through committees of the Labour Party National Executive, new policies for wide-ranging public-enterprise and planning controls gained the support both of ex-ministers and of trades unionists who had seen the failure of Keynesian planning result in the attempt of the 1964–70 Labour government to plan incomes and restrict key union freedoms through *In Place of Strife*. The case for changed social relations of production by major advances in industrial democracy gained ground through the Labour movement. The case was embodied in *Labour's Programme 1973* and carried in substance into the two 1974 manifestoes.

In the introductory essay to his volume *Socialism Now* (1974) Anthony Crosland castigated what he called 'the New Marxism' in the Labour Party and made an appeal for progressive Keynesianism of the old order. In government since 1974, a Cabinet representing mainly the Right of the parliamentary party, and to the Right of most constituency Labour parties, has drawn the teeth from the manifesto commitments through restricting the powers of the National Enterprise Board and the Planning Agreements system.

However, the Keynesian case for 'appropriate' exchange-rate changes plus rising public expenditure has taken a major pounding in government. Since 1971 sterling has been devalued by 40 per cent relative to the dollar and by 60 per cent relative to the Deutschmark, without the export-led growth which so massive a devaluation should have provoked even during a recession in overall world trade. A key reason lies in the transformed structure of supply and the dispropor-tionate multinational spread of British capital since 1950. If many of our leading firms followed through the devaluation and made a killing in export markets, they would mainly be reducing prices in markets where they already are direct producers. In public expenditure the Labour government is vainly trying to defend the value of sterling by cuts of a kind which probably would have been resisted by Keynes himself had he been alive to witness them. In his middle age he ad-vocated controls of foreign trade and a high degree of national protection as conditions for full employment, nearer to the Tribune group today than to Denis Healey's pre-Keynesian, monetarist policies.

Keynes is not here, and there is little point in hoping for a new Keynes to 'solve' Britain's economic problems. For the crisis of British capitalism needs wider-ranging economic, social and political change than ever Keynes considered necessary. It arguably demands fundamental and effectively revolutionary reforms in the balance of public and private power which only new public enterprise and social planning could ensure. Also, if the origins of the British crisis stem from a pre-Keynesian past, including the role of sterling as a world currency, and foreign investment patterns dating from the nineteenth century, the programme for fundamental transfor-mation of British capitalism embodied in Labour's *Programme 1976* shares key features with a continental Left to which Keynes in his own time was virtually blind.

In practice, Labour in government now is on a pre-Keyne-sian, monetarist tack. The TUC is divided, if not in ad-vocating medium-term policies for direct extension of public enterprise and planning, while accepting short-term con-straints on government room for manoeuvre. But the strategy of the Labour Party, like that of the other main parties of the West European Left, remains democratic socialist rather than Keynesian social democrat. If there is writing on the wall clear enough to be read for the future, it is no longer in Keynes's own powerful and idiosyncratic hand.

10 The Coming Corporatism

J. T. WINKLER

When the City of London starts volunteering earnest homilies about 'social responsibility in investment', then something terrible must surely be afoot. This is almost as portentous a reversal of the usual cliches as our trade-union celebrities issuing prolix justifications for a 'temporary suspension of free collective bargaining'. That simultaneously politicians have become rather more promiscuous than usual in abusing one another as 'fascists' is not, in itself perhaps, particularly noteworthy, but, when they start bothering to deny such accusations, then one is entitled to wonder whether something more is happening than just a change in fashions of political cant.

At the risk of becoming yet another prophet of a false twilight, I suggest that all this is more than standard, common-or-garden, run-of-the-mill hypocrisy. These are preliminary ideological accommodations to a fundamental change now taking place in Britain's economic system. We are moving beyond the resuscitated capitalism to which Keynes gave a kiss of life some years ago.

The operational Keynesianism, the Keynesianism that is written about in political weeklies as opposed to academic journals, consists of a small set of prescriptions about the role the state should play in the economy. To the extent that this Keynesianism-in-practice can be condensed into one sentence, it suggests that the state should manipulate taxation and public spending to regulate demand and thereby stabilise fluctuations in the trade cycle. Then businessmen, responding with only normal cupidity, will ensure that capitalism continues as before – for better or for worse, according to one's preferences in these matters. To be sure, these prescriptions are supported by a more extensive and complex theory about how economies work, which makes them seem plausible tactics of intervention. But when men get heated about 'Keynesianism' their concern is with public policy, not the realm of ideas.

The theme of this book is the passing of that approach to macro-economic management; the demise of the Keynesian era, and its aftermath. It is a serious and not just a rhetorical question to ask precisely what that means, particularly the bit about the aftermath. It means more than simply that Keynesian techniques are becoming discredited because they are increasingly failing to deliver what they promised – the control of unemployment, increased investment or a general effectiveness in dealing with the nation's economic problems. Such an interpretation is indisputable, but insufficient. It also becomes more hortative than descriptive when allied, as it usually is, to a remedial injunction that the state should reduce its intervention and trust more in the market or at least in monetarism. But, by any objective measure, the trend is in just the opposite direction. The Keynesian era is ending because the state is doing more things in the economy than Keynes recommended and there is a different logic to how these should be done.

In much contemporary political discussion, any and all increases in the state's economic activity are equated with the advance/incursion of socialism. This is a positive guarantee of misunderstanding what is happening in Britain in the 1970s. It is a derivation from the prevailing intellectual orthodoxy that there are only two alternatives for advanced industrial societies – capitalism or socialism. Change then is a matter of oscillation between them, with the level of state activity as the moving needle which indicates the trend (as in the present debate over public-expenditure cuts). A trifle more subtle discrimination is required. One must ask, what precisely is the state doing? What role is it playing in the economy? State activity can change qualitatively as well as quantitatively.

From our contemporary perspective, the most conspicuous new, non-Keynesian, state activity is the control of prices and incomes. There is virtually unanimous agreement from everyone in British public life (so spontaneously and manifestly self-interested that even the most dedicated conspiracy theorist need not posit collusion) that these controls are temporary. Politicians present them as crisis measures pending eventual return to (depending on the colour of their rosette) 'free enterprise' or 'free collective bargaining'. Prestigious economists and journalist cynics assure us, each in their own distinctive styles, that pent-up market forces and frustrated avarice always destroy controls anyhow. Administrative sophisticates observe that incomes policies keep breaking down in Phase Three.

This is all hortative flatulence, at best naïveté, at worst a lie. What is seldom remarked although equally observable is that incomes policies keep reformulating themselves. We have had them for most of the past decade, and the present 'voluntary' social contract is the seventh episode of pay pause/restraint/freeze/control since the war. These controls and others cited below will be permanent. They are part of a broader pattern of state intervention which has been developed pragmatically, incrementally and unarticulated, by governments of both parties.

The movement beyond Keynesianism began not with a burst of socialist appropriation, but with the acceptance by the Federation of British Industry and the Conservative government around 1960 of the need for some type of economic planning. This led to the establishment of the National Economic Development Organisation (NEDO), its four exercises in 'consenus planning', and on to the present attempts at both 'sectoral planning' and 'planning agreements'.

In the subsequent development, the highpoints (a literary metaphor only) have been two major attempts to regulate industrial relations, state management of industrial reorganisation and location, a proliferation of neo-mercantilist devices for export subsidisation and import-substitution, control, or increasing state provision of, industrial capital, and the increasing statutory or 'voluntary' controls over dividends, margins, rents and capital movements, as well as prices and incomes.

Equally important as these positive interventions have been the omissions and failures. Most notable, in the Labour phases, is the paucity of *new, intentional* nationalisation. Eight years of Wilson government have witnessed the renationalisation of steel and the planned acquisition of two industries (aircraft and shipbuilding) which the government effectively controlled already through a combination of subsidies, purchases and research grants. The rest is lame ducks and the sweet dreams of the National Executive Committee. As Andrew Shonfield has observed, 'One has to be very keen on being ideologically deceived to mistake [this] for socialist nationalisation.'

On the Tory side there developed during the Heath government a conspicuous unwillingness to accept the fluctuations of the market in their many manifestations – property speculation, retail inflation, militant collective bargaining, company failures, mass unemployment, capital exports or even the relative disinclination of industrialists to invest. This led to the interventionist U-turns and what Anthony Wedgwood Benn ungrudgingly called 'The most comprehensive armoury of government control that has ever been assembled for use over private industry.'

The central features in this stream of state activity over the past decade and a half have been that business has remained largely in private ownership, but the state has increasingly attempted to control its activity, and justified this in the name of the national interest. That is the pattern of recent state intervention. It is also a shorthand definition of corporatism. What is coming after the end of the Keynesian era is not socialism, but corporatism.

This is not a popular interpretation of what is happening in Britain. The reason is obvious, if not intellectually defensible. Despite the long history of corporatist socio-economic ideas in Europe, the term 'corporatism' today is inextricably associated in the public mind with the interwar fascist regimes. It has become a term of political abuse, not economic analysis. yet beneath the pejorative overtones, corporatism is a straightforward concept denoting a distinct type of economic system, one based on a combination of private ownership and state control. It contrasts with the private ownership and private control of capitalism and with socialism's state ownership and state control. Corporatism is the best *technical* description of the type of economic system toward which Britain is developing – but none of our mainstream political actors can afford to say so in public.

Politically, we are moving in this direction because the nation is no longer willing to tolerate 'the anarchy of the market' (to use the 1970s pejorative), is manifestly not attracted to comprehensive public ownership, yet finds Keynesian interventionist techniques increasingly unable to cope. The impulse to corporatism has been pragmatic, not ideological, adaptive problem-solving, not the intentional imposition of a coherent economic strategy; but the effects are no less fundamental for being unplanned and unannounced.

The logic of corporatist state intervention, the means by which it is is supposed to work, is completely different from Keynesian intervention. It is no longer just a matter of attempting to stabilise the aggregate economic environment, so that market processes can work with some semblance of normality. Rather, the corporatist state tries to exercise direct control over the internal decision-making of companies and over the bargaining strategies of unions.

The increasing state controls of recent years are thus more than just an extension or supplementation of Keynesian instruments of intervention. They are part of a qualitative change in the role that the state is playing in the British economy. It is no longer trying merely to facilitate, regulate, ameliorate, augment, stimulate, stabilise or support private economic activity; the state is trying to direct and control it – but without public appropriation.

This change of strategy is by no means complete, but the principle behind what is being attempted has recently become explicit in the parallel devices of the planning agreement and the social contract. The original concept of a planning agreement was much emasculated during its transition into law via the Industry Act 1975, but in theory it envisages regular, 'voluntary' agreements between major companies and the government covering prices, investment, technology, employment, exports, import-saving, industrial relations, product development, product quality and environmental protection. Translating these subject areas into the terms of business decision-making, a successfully concluded planning agreement would give the state *some* measure of control over what a company makes, how it makes it, to what standards, from what materials bought at what price, where it sells it for what price, how much capital is employed and how much labour; in short, some control over most of the important decisions a private owner or manager can make about his business.

If ever implemented as first envisaged, such agreements would significantly restrict the autonomy of private economic actors which is technically necessary for a *market* to operate; would transform *profit* from something maximisable into the residual cash left in the till after the agreement has been implemented; and would limit the right of *private property* holders to use or direct the use of what they own. In short, they would attack the three fundamental concepts of a capitalist economy.

We have yet to see the first planning agreement, but the control of unions has already gone somewhat further. In exchange for some limited promises on social policy which it has not wholly fulfilled, the 'voluntary' social contract has given the government considerable control over unions' bargaining goals for wages, pensions, fringe benefits and differentials – that is, over all the things in which their members are most interested. Far from establishing rule-by-the-TUC, the social contract is a very effective device for co-opting potential dissidents into government policy-making, which did not seem the most likely of developments in March 1974. It looks like becoming a permanent institution. How else would one interpret all the solemn rhetorical camouflage from union leaders lately about an 'orderly', 'phased' or 'planned' return to collective bargaining, with no relapse into a 'wages free-for-all'?

The gradual change from Keynesian to corporatist intervention involves a shift from aggregate or macro level regulation to the institutional or micro level, from general and indirect measures to specific and direct ones, beyond management of demand to the inclusion of supply as well, from a philosophy of fine tuning to one of control, from a supportive to a directive role for the state, from a strategy that works through the market to one that destroys the market – in sum, from a form of state intervention designed to sustain capitalism to one which would supplant it.

This evolution beyond Keynesianism is far from complete. Britain is not a corporatist economy today. Any government which seeks effective direction of its economy must also, to list only the most important areas, have some measure of control over the investment process, insulate its domestic institutions from the vicissitudes of international competition, and have some coherent national plan in terms of which to wield its instruments of intervention. These are the principal gaps in the apparatus of corporatist control today. They are also, thus, indicators of those areas where we may expect attempts at state intervention in the near future.

The process is already under way. We can see it most clearly in the rising debate over import controls and the bargaining with the Japanese over reciprocally acceptable levels of import penetration. It is also apparent in the tripartite planning exercise organised by NEDO for the industrial restructuring of thirty-nine manufacturing sectors; also in the slower-moving, coy debate between the City and Whitehall, begun by the Heath government during the property boom over 'socially responsible investment', which, de-euphemised, means getting the institutions to place their capital in accord with the government's priorities – at the moment, into manufacturing industry.

It is not part of the argument here that this development towards corporatist control is desirable or that it would be effective. The intent is analysis, not advocacy; to describe accurately a trend in public policy that has been going on for some time and to give it its proper name, a name which indicates how fundamental the changes would be if the trend continues. It is time we stopped discussing economic strategy as if we were building socialism, reforming capitalism, or just responding to a passing economic recession.

There is a very strong line of argument that, however accurate this description may be of past trends, these cannot continue much longer. Among political theorists, this is the notion of 'ungovernability', the idea that the government already suffers from such an 'overload' of demands upon it that it cannot adequately carry through its present tasks, much less take on new ones. Administrative pragmatists, suffused with that articulate, world-weary pessimism bred by long years in the civil service, observe that the state has never managed any real control over industry in the past and is unlikely to do much better in the future. On the Right, our present (Keynesian) crisis in budgetary policy is taken to show that there are limits to how much the state can spend; only so many lame ducks can be subsidised by the real producers. On the Left, this is known as 'the fiscal crisis of the state', that propping up a decreasingly profitable capitalism requires more revenue than the state can raise.

These financial arguments involve an assumption that the state makes its will effective through spending, that the exercise of state control necessitates transfer payments and therefore presumes substantial taxation. But government control can be increased without the government itself spending more money.

Price controls give the government considerable leverage over individual companies' *gross* revenues. The ability to adjust taxation (not just the corporation tax rate, of course, but allowances for depreciation and stock appreciation as well) gives the government some control over corporate *net* revenues. Together they constitute the upper and nether millstones with which, if you will pardon the metaphor, to grind down corporate liquidity. Their effectiveness was demonstrated in the liquidity crisis of 1974, when the corporate sector had a cash deficit of £3500 million. If the Labour government had been following a genuinely socialist policy, here was a unique opportunity for a vast extension of public ownership, by the unusual mechanism of driving British industry bankrupt. In fact, it acquired only three companies this way (Leyland, Ferranti, Herbert).

Rather, it reduced effective taxation and chose a corporatist strategy – which was articulated several times by the former Secretary of State for Prices and Consumer Affairs, Shirley Williams – of negotiating relaxations in price controls in return for companies' signing planning agreements or, more simply, increasing investment. Mrs Williams's successor, Roy Hattersley, recently affirmed the same approach: 'one should be less worried about the size of profits than the use of profits'. Here is a mechanism for putting pressure on individual private companies and controlling investment without transfers between public and private sectors.

Of course, government financial instruments are not limited to price controls and taxes. The government also has the power to purchase, lend, grant, borrow, subsidise, levy, license and charge for state-provided services. It has increasing controls over wages, dividends, rents, credit, interest

rates, capital movements and tariffs/imports. Some of these
devices can be applied only to broad business categories,
others to specific companies.

The corporatist financial strategy consists in the state's us-
ing these multiple controls to modulate corporate revenue as a
bargaining lever for extracting all manner of 'agreements'
from industry. Essentially, it is the bartering of cash flow for
conformity to public policy. The instruments for such a
strategy are now in place; all that is wanting for its implementation is a co-ordination mechanism for their coherent
application. The logic of the strategy is that it works through
the internal financing of individual companies and not, in the
Keynesian manner, through manipulation of national
aggregates.

The same approach may be taken to personal as well as to
corporate incomes, and here too the corporatist control over
unions is somewhat further advanced. As Turner and Wilkin-
son have repeatedly demonstrated, previous governments,
both Labour and Conservative, have attempted retroactively
to claw back, through increases in direct or indirect taxes and
reductions in welfare transfers, what they have seen as inflationary wage settlements. In summer 1976, the Chancellor
shifted (successfully) to an anticipatory strategy of bargaining
tax cuts for union agreement to tighter income control. Essentially, he was bartering real income for conformity to public
policy. It was a historic shift in British government strategy –
towards corporatism. In both sectors, price and wage controls
over gross incomes are essential to the whole approach. They
are not Canute-like gestures against a temporary phase of
world inflation; they are permanent features of a corporatist
financial strategy.

As both these examples make clear, corporatist 'state control' is not an authoritarian or bureaucratic imposition from
above, but the outcome of continuous, often covert, bargaining
between the state and private economic groups possessing real
power. There will always be compromise, but over time, as the
state adds new instruments of control and increases the effectiveness of their application, the prospect is for an incremental
expansion of the state's control over the economy and a corresponding diminution in the realm of private discretion.

It will be a gradual, unheralded, perhaps even largely unnoticed process, because what we are going through is a slow shifting of the boundaries of both permissible and mandatory action by the state, morally justified in terms of an ambiguous and changing 'national interest'. But at some stage, in a crude sense, the economic initiative will have transferred from private groups to the state and we shall thereby have crossed over that conceptual line between a Keynesian variant of capitalism and its aftermath, corporatism. This is not a determinist prediction; in political economy other alternatives are always available. But it is the most probable line of development. If the trend of the past fifteen years continues, the British economy will be essentially corporatist before the end of the 1980s.

11 Keynes and the Developing World

HARRY G. JOHNSON

Keynes was a British economist and economic policy operator, concerned with the economic and policy problems of the British economy, of Britain and the European economies in the World War I reconstruction period, and of Britain and the world financial system in the World War II reconstruction period, but always primarily with Britain. His only major work in what would now be called 'development economics' was *Indian Currency Reform*, based on a plan worked out at the India Office and researched from there (he later used pressure of academic business to refuse an official mission to India). His only major policy contribution as a British official involved a clear case of imperial colonial exploitation: arranging to buy for British consumers in the First World War a surplus of Indian wheat available at a price below the world market price because the India Office had held the price down with the aid of an export embargo to prevent the Indian peasant from becoming unwarrantedly affluent. It is true that towards the end of his career he publicly favoured international commodity agreements, a fact now being used to give intellectual support to the demands for 'a new international economic order'; but that is a culturally insignificant part of his literary legacy to modern economic culture.

If 'development' is defined in a broad, economic rather than political, sense, as economic growth, its sources, and policies for promoting it, Keynes certainly had ideas on it that were influential. But those ideas were social, a-scientific, and distracting in the worst sense of the term. They derived from, and were conditioned by, the opulent euphoria of deeply class-organised late nineteenth-century Britain, compounded with the contempt of the educated chosen for a career of responsible social management – the don and the civil servant – for the intellectually inferior who live by working and by making money from organising the work of others. In economic theory they were shaped and sharpened by the principle of Occam's Razor, on which the lazy economic theorist frequently cuts his own scientific throat – in economics, the principle that everything can be related to one key macro-economic variable, a principle which unites (at least in their worst moments or in their vulgar followers) Marx (the rate of profit), Keynes (fixed capital investment), and Milton Friedman (the quantity of money).

These ideas led Keynes to three views: that, if the British economy were properly managed, it could accumulate all the capital it could use in a generation or so; that entrepreneurs would happily perform their entrepeneurial functions for modest after-tax incomes; and that policy directed at fixed capital investment was the key to full employment and social bliss. The first view has been decently forgotten by active economists in this more democratic age of 'rising aspirations'; but its simple substitute has been the view that subsidisation of fixed investment is the key to the promotion of growth, with the only room for debate being between emphasising the subsidies themselves, or providing them indirectly via demand pressure, and, if the latter, whether via domestic inflation or via currency undervaluation. (The recent book by Bacon and Eltis typifies the Keynesian 'fixed investment' tradition; Lord Kaldor has long been an advocate of the policy of deliberate undervaluation of the pound, the centre-piece of current British socialist policy.) This emphasis on fixed industrial investment, and on demand policies and subsidies to encourage it, has implied the exclusion from Keynesian thinking of both the old English classical and neo-classical emphasis on human motivations which encourage or discourage investment and innovation, and the modern American emphasis on a completely different concept of 'capital', a concept which includes 'human capital' or ability, training, and self-improvement as a major form of capital and assigns to the accumulation of education and knowledge a major role in economic growth.

With regard to the narrower concept of 'development', the economic growth (especially in *per capita* terms) of the poor regions of the world, Keynes's intellectual influence fell to be exercised through his disciples. But the influence has been great – and, again, distracting, in the pejorative sense. That influence can be associated with two theoretical concepts, each identifiable with a still-living first-generation disciple of the master; and, understandably, both ideas have been especially influential in the former British colonial region of the Indian sub-continent.

The first, and simpler, idea is that of 'disguised unemployment', attributable to Joan Robinson. The concept, in its original context and formulation, was indisputably relevant and useful: it is simply the idea that in times of mass unemployment many of the formerly appropriately employed turn, not to the dole (or unemployment insurance and assistance), but to lesser types and degrees of economic activity that fail to use, or to compensate appropriately, the productive abilities they possess, but which do keep them out of the official measurements of the total of unemployed. (An American economist, Arthur Okun, gained international fame for a more sophisticated and quantified version of the same idea, elevated to the status of 'Okun's Law'.) Where it proved superficially plausible, but fundamentally misleading, was in its transmogrification into a description, analysis and policy principle for the poor countries, with their characteristic preponderance of people in rural districts who seem to do little or nothing to contribute to agricultural output. The notion that there exist masses of 'disguised unemployed' people leads easily into the idea that 'development' involves merely the mobilisation and transfer of these presumably costless productive resources into economic activities, primarily investment or industrial production, at an obvious and virtually costless social economic gain. What is required to realise this gain is, gratifyingly enough, merely cleverness on the part of the economist in outwitting the stupidity of the competitive system, and determination by the political leaders in generating the social will needed to implement the appropriate economic policies.

Tremendous efforts have been made, notably in India, to define operationally and to measure the amount of 'disguised unemployment', and to develop and incorporate into policy and into cost-benefit analysis of policy proposals and projects the implicit difference between the money and the social (alternative-opportunity) cost of labour; and also to discredit the 'neo-classical' alternative approach, represented particularly by T. W. Schultz's *Transforming Traditional Agriculture*. Schultz argued that farmers are efficient in exploiting the technology available to them, that the phenomena of 'disguised unemployment' are symptoms of a low-productivity technology, and that conversion to a superior technology involves an interconnected complex of changes involving not merely the technology itself but also the supply of appropriate inputs (fertiliser, water, seeds, pesticides), including the education of the farmer himself. Schultz was clearly right, as centuries of agricultural economic history have shown; but the city man's contempt for the farmer, and the Keynesian belief that there is something wrong with the economy that is attributable to the competitive system and that could be understood and set right by a feat of economic brilliance have remained in control of the theory and policy of economic development.

The second extremely influential Keynesian idea was the so-called Harrod–Domar equation, the centre-piece of R. F. Harrod's extension of the Keynesian model for the explanation of short-run unemployment in a capitalist system into a model of self-sustaining economic growth in such a system. Briefly, the equation states that the growth of fixed capital will generate just sufficient increased sales and profits to justify the investment involved in increasing the capital stock if g, the growth rate, is equal to s, the proportion of full-employment-of-capital output saved, divided by k, the normal ratio of capital stock to output. Harrod's own interest lay in the question of whether this growth rate, which he assumed would satisfy entrepreneurs and keep them investing for further growth, would be lower or higher than the 'natural' rate of growth, made possible by the natural growth of population and the rate of technical advance: if lower, there would be a growing reserve army of the unemployed; if higher, the economy would encounter bottlenecks of labour supply that would throw it back into recession. But the equation provided a framework for planned economic growth, since the attainable growth rate would depend on the proportion of total production that the planners could extract from the economy as saving, and the amount of additional output that could be obtained per unit of investment by the planners' choice of projects (the capital–output ratio).

The Harrod–Domar equation had the important advantage of concentrating on the central structure of the development-planning problem, and emphasising the requirement of overall consistency in the planning process. But it automatically involved the same error as the 'disguised unemployment' concept, through its emphasis on physical investment and implicit disregard of the availability of labour, and especially skilled and technical and scientific labour, to work with the material capital created by investment. (Underlying the process of growth through investment is, of course, a complex of other requirements, reaching into such areas as political stability, the rule of law in contractual arrangements, and social approval or toleration of the receipt of profits from successful investment.)

The role of labour supply as a constraint on production similar to the constraint imposed by the stock of capital was only gradually recognised. Initially, recognition took the form of distinguishing between average and marginal or 'incremental' capital–output ratios, on the grounds that the average capital–output ratio includes the productive contributions not only of capital but also of the other productive resources used. Subsequently, it took the form of large-scale exercises in 'manpower planning', i.e. forecasting the additional supplies of skilled labour of various types that would be required by the planned growth of industry and its material capital equipment in the economy, and planning the expansion of educational facilities and the growth of their intakes of students to produce skilled labour in the numbers that would be needed to fit the planned growth of capital. This effort was, however, as economically poorly grounded in economics as previous exercises in planning in terms of physical capital only had been. The fundamental error was in assuming both that there is a fixed ratio between total output and the labour of each specification required to co-operate with material capital in producing the output, and that labour skills are a form of highly specific capital equipment that can be produced only by a formal educational process applied to the human raw material at a particular age of presumably transient malleability. In fact, people are quite capable of devising informal techniques for acquiring particular productive skills if there are strong-enough economic incentives for doing so. On the other hand, as the evident failure of British educational policy in its post-Sputnik emphasis on producing a new type of technologically-oriented Englishman has shown, people are not stupid enough – if the evidence of their own eyes is that the arts man has a more rewarding career than the scientist, and that the lawyer enjoys a higher standard of living than the sanitary engineer – to embark on forms of industrial and technological training which government claims will be required in future.

Both of the concepts just discussed – disguised unemployment, and the Harrod–Domar equation – while not of Keynes's own coining, are essentially Keynesian both by direct discipleship and by intellectual affinity with the concentration on fixed capital investment as the prime economic mover in the *General Theory* (and significant strands in his earlier work, including at some stretch of the imagination his conviction that Germany could not possibly pay the reparations demanded of her after the First World War – European and especially German experience after the Second World War showed conclusively that, provided its stock of human capital and the mechanisms for generating it remained basically intact, a country could recover fairly quickly from large-scale destruction of its material capital stock).

No mention has been made thus far of the second of Keynes's leading ideas mentioned above, that entrepreneurs will (should? should be expected to?) perform their mundane tasks of business management, innovation and risk-taking for relatively small rewards. It is, in fact, extremely difficult to separate the influence of the urbane, civilised, and patrician view of Keynes on this score from, on the one hand, that of the welfare-economics tradition set by his teacher A. C. Pigou and his mentor Alfred Marshall, and, on the other hand, that attribution of entrepreneurial decisions to unexplained but vaguely contemptible 'animal spirits' and that denial of any economic justification to profits, spiced with Marxist class hatred of the capitalists as a class, that has come to characterise 'Keynesian economics' as taught by Keynes's disciples at Oxford and Cambridge. Keynes himself is probably blameless, in the sense that anyone confronted directly with Keynes's own statement of his views would recognise and discard them for what they are, a Victorian *fin-de-siècle* intellectual period piece. But 'Keynesian economics' has had a great deal to do with the emergence of development economics. It began with the faith that capital accumulation in the form of planned industrialisation would quickly result in the closing of the gap between the poor or less developed countries and the rich or 'advanced developed' countries. Becoming disillusioned with the social results of this kind of development, and particularly its failure to reduce economic inequalities *within* the developing countries, it culminated in some vocal advocacy of abandoning the goal of 'development' in favour of a more just and equitable society. That evolution itself is easily understood, as a consequence of exaggerated expectations generated by the Keynesian concentration on fixed capital investment; the predictable effects in increasing the more blatant appearances of inequality of methods of capital accumulation that were bound to concentrate ownership of capital in the hands of the few possessing scarce managerial skills or the political skill to cajole monopoly privileges and subsidies out of the machinery of centralised government; and the Keynesian failure to appreciate the effects of rapid population growth in soaking up the gains from capital accumulation and technological improvement that would otherwise accrue to labour in the form of increasing real wages and real income *per capita*.

In summary, Keynes himself was little concerned with the problem of economic development; and, to the extent that he was so concerned, his embeddedness in the English class society led him to regard it as a problem readily and quickly solvable by a modicum of additional capital accumulation. His disciples, however, provided extensions of his ideas that seemed readily applicable to the by-then more serious problem of promoting economic development in the poorer parts of the world. But the apparent advance of knowledge was illusory. Their failure lay in turning simplifications of reality that were appropriate to the problem of mass unemployment with which Keynes was concerned – notably, the crucial importance of the level of fixed capital investment, given the implicit assumption that savings behaviour had become habitual, and the availability of labour in the right quantity and skill-mix to man the capital equipment – into unverified assumptions about the facts of a different reality.

12 Keynes and the 'Pax Americana'

DAVID P. CALLEO

Like the Impressionists, Keynes has been going out of fashion. Even admiring critics, while acknowledging his immense influence in shaping and stabilising the post-war capitalist restoration, now find strains in his thought which are believed to be undermining that restoration. Thus Keynesian prescriptions are seen as a transitory rather than durable resolution for the problems of modern capitalism.

Critics single out two major elements in Keynes's thinking; his faith in an enlightened and public-spirited technocracy to 'manage' the economy, and his emphasis on full employment and consumption as opposed to stability and saving. These two Keynesian preoccupations, it is said, have translated into governmental policies which have gradually undermined the foundations of economic equilibrium. The emphasis on manipulation has steadily overwhelmed those market mechanisms which sustain equilibrium naturally, while the technocratic management, which is supposed to have done the manipulating, has proved incompetent to do so. Why?

In the national economy under Keynesian influence, it is said, economics and politics inextricably entwine, to the detriment of both. As the state has tried to take over the market, so interest groups have tried to take over the state. In democracies particularly, Keynes's mandarins are left with little room for manoeuvre. With the market suppressed and the élite overwhelmed, no effective check resists the clamouring interests. Economics becomes 'politicised', and there is not a political balance sufficient to preserve a common national interest in equilibrium. The result, supposedly, is persistent inflation, increasingly marked by shrinking investment and growing unemployment.

These fatal Keynesian predilections are traced to Keynes's

own cultural and social background. His faith in technocracy over the market reflects, it is said, the high-minded confidence of a great governing class, still living in a paternalistic age. His emphasis on consumption over saving reflects the self-destructive reaction of that class against the Victorian morality which gave it discipline and legitimacy.

Whatever the justice of these criticisms in other respects, they themselves suffer from a significant flaw. For they blame the national 'failures' of Keynesian policies on domestic factors, while ignoring the vital international dimension. The 'Age of Keynes' has also been, after all, the *Pax Americana*. And Keynesian national economic policies, whatever their own tendencies, have had to be conducted within an international order which has, itself, certain definite tendencies which it transmits to national systems. Among these tendencies is a strong inclination toward inflation as well as the progressive disposition to rob national governments of the very means of intervention and planning which Keynes's domestic prescriptions presupposed.

Keynes, of course, was well aware of the possible tension between managing successfully the domestic economy and participating in a disordered international system. It forms a recurring preoccupation throughout his writing. But to what extent is today's disordered international system itself Keynesian in inspiration? The question raises interesting issues, not only about the nature and origin of the present world system, but also about the inner character and consistency of Keynes's economic theory.

Keynes's great influence on the present international system is obvious. Keynesian ideas permeate much of contemporary economic analysis and even more of contemporary economic policy. Not only have numerous Keynesian followers been among the managers of the post-war international order, but Keynes himself was a major protagonist in the Anglo-Saxon negotiations which planned it. The Bretton Woods Conference of 1944, out of which emerged the International Monetary Fund, was essentially a struggle between Keynes's British draft and White's American scheme. The struggle, it might be argued, was more apparent than real. Both were, in essence, variations of Keynes's earlier ideas about a supranational system to manage the world money supply, ideas found at length, for example, in the *Treatise on Money,* published in 1930. Thus, it can easily be said, the post-war international order, like the domestic, bears the mark of Keynes.

But it may also be said that, however much his theories set the frame for interallied planning, his own role toward the end of the war was not an altogether happy one and his misgivings about the future were formidable and growing. War had not made Keynes forget the depression and the terrible danger for liberal societies of an ailing capitalism. He was torn between his old enthusiasm for international economic management and his keen appreciation of Britain's new weakness. The former drew him toward partnership with America in building a new order; the latter made him fear for Britain's influence and prosperity within that order. He thus approached the Anglo-American economic negotiations with two great concerns: fear of a return to the age of deflation and fear for Britain's own terrible weakness. A post-war monetary order was needed, Keynes realised, which did not mandate a general return to the deflation and unemployment of the inter-war period and which, moreover, would give Britain vast credits to finance her own difficult post-war adjustment. The two preoccupations merged in his proposal for a clearing union – a sort of world central bank with arrangements not only to create international money to finance disequilibria, but also to press surplus as well as deficit countries to adjust their economies. With this scheme, Keynes hoped to preserve equilibrium without unemployment, while avoiding for Britain a period of perilous economic misery.

No one knew better than Keynes just how desperate post-war Britain's economic condition would be, a condition far worse than before the war. Overseas investments were gone, huge foreign debts had been contracted and many old markets were lost. Converting industry to peacetime and regaining old markets in the face of American competition would be extremely difficult. The pre-war Commonwealth preferential system, which had once provided shelter, was seriously eroded and the Americans seemed determined relentlessly to destroy it altogether.

A mind as mordant and sensitive as Keynes's no doubt felt the full irony of Britain's predicament. Britain had been brave and steadfast. Nazi Germany had got neither quarter nor compromise. No doubt, World War II was Britain's finest hour. In the end, however, Britain had won the victory but not the war. For, in effect, Britain and her Empire were now completely dependent upon the Americans. As it was Churchill's destiny to fight the war, it was Keynes's fate to get the bill. Thus the drama of Keynes's last years: the peerless economist, representing the best of a great intellectual and political tradition, coming to Washington to beg a place for Britain in America's new world.

The war's ruinous cost to Britain was, of course, predictable. Chamberlain appears to have understood well enough what another war would mean. Hitler had always expected a British deal – to avoid just the outcome Keynes ultimately faced. Why, Hitler constantly asked, should Britain bleed to death to deliver the world to the Americans? Why hadn't there been peace in 1941, after Britain had beaten Germany in the air and Italy in the Mediterranean? As he sat in his bunker, awaiting the end, Hitler consoled himself; 'Churchill by refusing to come to terms with me, has condemned his country to a policy of suicide' (*The Testament of Adolf Hitler* (London: Cassell, 1961), p. 30).

While no one need wonder that Britain doubted the possibility of an accord with Hitler's Germany, and preferred dependence on Roosevelt's America, British statesmen had ample reason for apprehension about what would happen after the war. For more than a half-century, American imperialists had looked forward to inheriting Britain's world position. The Anglo-American financial and trade warfare of the 1920s and 1930s, which had made Chamberlain so reluctant to place Britain's safety in American hands, was only a recent memory. American aid throughout the war had been hedged with restrictions which weakened Britain's future independence.

The more sanguine among Keynes's British contemporaries found refuge in fantasy. America, guided by Britain, was going to re-establish the liberal world of the last century, its harsher features suitably modified by Keynesian palliatives. The United States would contribute the power and the money; Britain would provide the brains and the banks. Hence, Britain's future lay neither with the eroding Com-

monwealth, nor with the new Europe rising from the ashes,
but in a special relationship with America to rebuild the
nineteenth century. A transatlantic Greater Britain would
rescue the world from Darwin and restore the age of Cobden.
The dream persists to this day. But Britain was not able to
play the role of junior partner, and the attempt has done her
harm. Britain's effort, moreover, was not much appreciated in
America. On the contrary, a weak but pretentious Britain
spoiled the logic of hegemony and proved a sort of American
Achilles heel. A weak pound discredited reserve currencies
and pointed up the dollar's own vulnerability. A British
nuclear force led to a French and, from the start, made a
serious policy against non-proliferation impossible.

Whatever the expectations about 'special relationship'
among his contemporaries, Keynes himself seems to have been
sceptical and ambivalent. All the courtesy, respect and personal affection which Americans like Acheson lavished upon
Keynes could not hide the obvious truth. The new age was to
be the *Pax Americana*. The Americans had the power and the
money and they expected to call the tune. The American-
inspired arrangements for the future, moreover, showed a disconcerting tendency toward policing the domestic economies
of others. When the veil of politeness was pulled aside, as at
the first IMF Conference at Savannah in 1944, where
American power revealed itself in the particularly graceless
form of Treasury Secretary Vinson, Keynes must have seen
well enough what had happened to Britain. He carried off his
role as chief negotiator for the American loan with brilliance
and aplomb. But it was not a position likely to nourish illusions of grandeur.

Time has made us forget the sharpness of the
Anglo-American economic conflicts of the early post-war
period. Nothing like them was seen again until the rise of
Gaullist France. What finally resolved this early transatlantic
conflict was the Cold War. Keynes simply died too soon to
enjoy it. He never lived to see Congress ratify the British loan,
the quest which had absorbed his final energies. Significantly,
ratification came shortly after Churchill's 'iron curtain'
speech. The determining sentiment in Congress was fear of
Stalin rather than admiration for Keynes. In due course, fear
prompted that bonanza of American aid which doubtless

would have exceeded Keynes's greatest hopes – the Marshall Plan, NATO and the Korean rearmament.

But if the Cold War resolved many immediate problems, it also confirmed that America's role would be far more hegemonic than the multilateral arrangements of Bretton Woods had envisioned. The arrangements Keynes and White had so patiently negotiated remained mostly imaginary. American money, catalysed by the Cold War, financed Europe's recovery and rearmament. Europe became first a protectorate, then feared becoming a subsidiary. The dependent relationship had inevitable monetary consequences. As the dollar gap of the 1940s became the dollar glut of the 1960s, the world gradually discovered that it was firmly on the dollar standard. Bretton Woods, it turned out, was meant only for lesser powers. The United States, thanks politically to its protector's role and technically to the dollar's position as principal reserve currency, never accepted multilateral discipline for itself. Instead, the United States has remained in deficit for the better part of three decades. When the rest of the world finally balked at accepting more surplus dollars, the United States simply floated. And floating has proved no more constraining on American monetary freedom than the stillborn Bretton Woods system. For a depreciated dollar is, in fact, a greater threat to Europe than to America.

In short, the real post-war monetary system is far more genuinely imperial than anything imagined at Bretton Woods. Those who thought the United States would simply take over Britain's role before World War I, and preside as 'manager' over a Keynesian version of the old liberal world order, greatly underestimated and misunderstood American power. For the United States has come to exercise a very different sort of hegemony over the world economy from Britain's before 1914. Britain then, despite her informal managerial role, was a power not so much greater than her continental rivals. In the end, the disciplines of the gold standard, as they had evolved, applied to Britain as well as to France or Germany. And Britain was so dependent upon the world economy that international considerations perforce weighed heavily upon her domestic policy. The United States, by contrast, is a vast, semi-autarchic superpower. America's role as 'system manager' is not inevitably the central preoccupation of

American politics. For the United States is not among the first to suffer from mismanagement of the world system, but among the last.

To be sure, things have not turned out so badly. This post-war *Pax Americana* has had many obvious advantages. Even an American may permit himself to say that his country's hegemony has, on the whole, been intelligent and generous. Despite the unceasing talk of the Soviet threat, European countries have known a prosperous security rare in their modern histories. But, unfortunately, perhaps, the system has not proved stable – above all in the monetary sphere. The world has been flooded with excess dollars. A vast pool of offshore money constitutes just that kind of volatile international capital that Keynes long ago saw as a major threat to the rational managing of domestic economies. Predictably, this prolonged disequilibrium has led to a breakdown of stable parities, relentless inflation and, in general, a more and more erratic world economy. Nor is it surprising, under these circumstances, that conflicts over income distribution increasingly unsettle national societies, strain democratic political systems and render the gentle Keynesian techniques of national economic management increasingly ineffective.

If Keynes were alive today, what would he think of the present international system? The question is obviously too complex, subtle and hypothetical. But a few observations may stimulate further thought. Clearly, the present system has many features of Keynesian inspiration. But its mode of management is not, one suspects, what Keynes had in mind. And Keynes did, after all, believe in equilibrium and social stability. He was not an amoral technocrat serving power with a bag of tricks. Above all he wished to achieve and preserve a humane version of English liberal society. His writings suggest a reasonable awareness of the dangers of inflation for social stability. But, understandably, inflation was not his primary preoccupation during the inter-war period.

Keynes was, moreover, keenly aware of the tension between successful economic management on a national scale and participation in a world system. Throughout much of his life, he urged Britain to cut loose from the existing international system in order to give priority to domestic needs. In today's situation, Keynes might well counsel reform not so much for domestic economies as for an international order that makes rational domestic management increasingly difficult. Keynes, of course, longed for that international order which might reconcile national and international stability. But, when it came to a conflict, his mind turned to national protection. He would not, I suspect, have been enthusiastic about an international system which was both unmanageable and highly integrated.

If the arrangements at Bretton Woods were Keynesian, and have 'failed', does their failure indicate some fundamental weakness in Keynes's grasp of economic or political realities? While it is sometimes argued that Bretton Woods made inadequate provision to compel adjustment, it seems idle, in view of the prevailing circumstances, to blame the post-war system's shortcomings on institutional technicalities. A more convincing criticism may be made of Keynes's grasp of political realities. Did he, for instance, place too much reliance upon goodwill and consultation among high-minded transatlantic élites and pay too little attention to cultivating a genuine balance of power? Was this faith in a special relationship between British and American élites a particular case of a general Keynesian naïveté about technocrats, as mentioned at the outset? For the reasons I have been urging, it seems unreasonable to single out Keynes for naïveté about the special relationship. It has been a British national failing, closely related, I suspect, to a lingering enthusiasm for imperialism. Somehow the British seem to have convinced themselves that a happy world requires a hegemonic master, that they had been that master in the last century and that it had become their duty to make way for their chosen successor in this. Thus the imperial fantasy was projected on to the Americans. But even in abdication, it was thought, Britain was to retain a major role. The new imperial élite would have to be trained by the old and, as a consequence, new British influence would effectively substitute for old British power.

Hindsight is unkind to these illusions. Yet they persist. As Marcello de Cecco notes in Chapter 3 above, Keynes began life as a Roman – a 'history maker' – and ended as an Italian – a 'history taker'. The shift proved too great for the British political imagination to absorb in Keynes's generation. Hence the vicarious imperialism. It took friendly Americans, like

Acheson, to tell the British to get on with a new role worthy of their genius. The beginning of success, I expect, will come when imperialism ceases to bemuse and the British rediscover the balance of power. For Burke and Acton are probably more relevant to today's world than Hobbes, and certainly more appropriate to Britain's own post-war position.

As for Keynes's shortcomings, it bears remembering that Britain had few options. Keynes did what had to be done with the Americans in 1944. Britain's subsequent European policy is another matter.

As Keynes was reminded at the end of his life, the economic order is made by power. Until there is a more settled and perhaps more natural balance of power within the capitalist world, economic equilibrium – national or international – will continue to be elusive. That is a lesson Keynes may have learned too late to impart to his disciples.

13 The Keynesian Era in Perspective

GEOFFREY BARRACLOUGH

There are still people today – there always will be – who cherish the illusion, as plenty of others did in the 1920s, of a speedy return to 'normalcy', by which they mean a return to the continuing 'self-sustaining' growth of the 1960s. But every sensible person knows that we stand at the end of an era in economic history. It is usually called the Keynesian era, but whether this is the right description is a different question. Every age, it seems, needs its father-figure, to praise or to abuse; and John Maynard Keynes has been saddled with many things for which he was not responsible. Marx in his old age said he was no Marxist; and Keynes, if he were alive to-day, or even if he had been alive in 1960, might have come to feel himself no Keynesian. 'The Keynesian Revolution' and 'the Keynesian era' are clichés which require analysis, not parrot-like repetition.

In saying this, I have no wish to engage in one of those sterile semantic debates so beloved of academics. There is no smoke without a fire, and Robert Skidelsky is right in saying that we cannot draw a hard-and-fast line separating Keynes from the Keynesians. What Keynes contributed above all else to the Keynesian armoury was the fearsome weapon of aggregate demand management. What he did not know, and could not know, was the uses to which this weapon would be put. Nor could he know that a short-term remedy for a situation of chronic under-production and unemployment would be turned into a magic long-term formula for continuous growth.

The key to Keynes's thought, and by implication to the Keynesian era, is his famous remark, 'In the long run we are all dead.' The Keynesians are concerned with the long run; Keynes was not. When he published the *General Theory* in 1936 there was enough to worry about in the short run. What Keynes was propounding, as the title of his famous treatise explicitly states, was a *General Theory of Employment*, not a sovereign remedy for all and sundry economic ills. (The full title of the work is, of course, *The General Theory of Employment, Interest and Money;* but the purpose of Keynes' discussion of interest and money is to provide a theoretical underpinning, sophisticated enough to convince the economic pundits, for his arguments about employment. Employment, or rather unemployment, is his central theme and evident concern.) It was written, in other words, for the 1930s, and not for the 1960s or 1970s. Keynes knew that, in the practical world, the solution of one problem – in this case unemployment – is simply the beginning of other problems. Whether, if he had not died prematurely in 1946, he would have turned his mind to these other problems, we do not know. But Joseph Davis reports him saying 'emphatically', at a dinner in Washington in 1944 or 1945, that in the post-war world the danger from inflation would be greater than the danger from depression. If true, this prescient remark suggests that he might have been less than enthusiastic about the so-called Keynesian revolution, then getting under way.

Keynesianism, as it developed after 1946, drew on Keynes, but it also drew on other sources. There is no need to describe the stages – beginning, it is generally agreed, with Harrod's famous 'Essay in Dynamic Theory' of 1939 – by which Keynes's short-term analysis of a particular historical situation was turned into a long-term recipe for steady growth. This is familiar territory for economists. But the real culprits (though that is not the epithet they would have used) were the bright boys on the banks of the Charles river, who reduced Keynesian economics to a bag of tools, available to any graduate of Harvard Business School or the Massachusetts Institute of Technology, among which they could pick and choose at will, selecting those devices which suited their purpose and discarding the rest. They were the progenitors (illegitimate, as might be expected) of vulgar or commercialised Keynesianism, which they fathered on neo-classicism. The result, in Robert Lekachman's words, was 'a brew of Keynes and Adam Smith that displeases even the brewers'. It was a mixture of incompatible elements that was bound in the end to blow up in the alchemists' faces.

In retrospect, the surprising thing is how long the explosion was in coming. To begin with, as we all know, and for many years, the 'new economics' (as it soon came to be called) appeared to be succeeding beyond the boldest expectation. Whether it could have done otherwise in the circumstances – given, that is to say, the pent-up demand, the needs of post-war reconstruction, and the like – is another question. It was also carried on the back of a major wave of technological innovation, paid for happily by wartime expenditure and readily available for large-scale exploitation; and, when the momentum seemed to flag, and pessimists predicted a repetition of the 1929 slump, the Korean war arrived like a *deus ex machina* to keep the indices moving in the right direction. But it would be wide of the mark to present the post-war expansion as simply a combintion of luck and circumstance. If, for the industrialised countries (but not for the world as a whole), the fifteen years between 1948 and 1963 were a time of unparalleled growth, there is no doubt that the commitment to growth and full employment, and the realisation that government could influence both, were a major factor; and this commitment had its root in Keynes. Of course, it was not maintained consistently; but it is what we mean by the Keynesian Revolution.

Granted the Keynesian premises, the message, translated into the language of vulgar Keynesianism, was simple in the extreme. Put crudely, it was that any consumption which maintained aggregate demand at a level at which resources would be fully employed was good. Keynes had dealt a death blow at the old ideals of prudence and saving; consumption was the new watchword. Of course, this simplification is unfair to the distinguished economists who joined the President's Council of Economic Advisers or who operated in Whitehall. But it was welcome news to the manufacturers for whom the business schools catered, particularly to the manufacturers of products which no one in his right mind would want to consume, unless he were brainwashed (as he was) by the media.

Of course, there was more to it than this. The crude calculations of the marketplace are always with us. The foundations of the Keynesian era were not only economic but also psychological and political. Today it is easy to forget how profoundly attitudes – even economists' attitudes – were influenced in the 1950s by the Cold War. It was not for nothing that Walt Rostow's once famous book, *The Stages of Economic Growth,* was sub-titled 'A Non-Communist Manifesto'. Politically, it was necessary to show that capitalism could deliver the goods. Psychologically, the pre-war depression cast a long shadow. Contraction, or slump, were still the great enemies. Expansion was assumed to be benign, particularly if the gushing waters could be controlled by a spigot from the Keynesian bag of tools. But the great, overriding object was to keep the wheels turning. When, during the so-called 'Eisenhower recession' of 1957-8, the President took it upon himself to advise the public to buy, and was asked what, he answered, 'Anything!'

Underlying the President's advice was the familiar Keynesian axiom that, if demand is right, supply will look after itself, businessmen will invest in new capital equipment, the economy will grow, there will be more for all, and some at least will 'trickle down' from the rich at the top to the poor at the bottom. In all this Keynes himself was certainly not innocent. He was more concerned with the size than with the nature of spending, and perhaps in the 1930s sheer spending was good enough. By the end of the 1960s, after a spending spree unparalleled in history, it was not. By then, as Galbraith has pointed out, the affluent society was cluttered up, beyond the point of no return, with non-essentials. It may have been good for business, producing one gadget after another, from transistor radios to electric razors; but it is another question whether it was good for anyone else, or even whether in the long run it was good for business. But businessmen, like Keynes, are not very interested in the long run.

The reason why it was not good for business or for anyone else was, quite simply, that in the long run it could not last. The cardinal sin of the self-styled Keynesians was surely their insistence that it could, the blithe self-confidence with which they proclaimed that Keynesian economics had overcome the age-old cycle of boom and slump. Keynes himself, so far as I am aware, never suggested anything of the sort; but the notion was so congenial that it had only to be propounded to be believed. When – in 1968, of all years! – Andrew Shonfield predicted that 'a major set-back of Western economic growth seems on balance unlikely', he was only echoing common opinion. Anti-cyclical policy, the magic of the Keynesian 'multiplier', and the other brightly furbished tools, would do the trick. We know to our cost that they didn't. Keynes, Joan Robinson tells us, used to say, 'The long period is a subject for undergraduates.' He couldn't have been more wrong. What has happened is that the long-term cycle, thrown out of Keynes's front door, has come flying back through the window - and broken a lot of china in the process.

We speak airily of a 'Keynesian era', but the economic history of the thirty years between 1945 and 1975 could almost be written – almost but not quite – without mentioning Keynes's name. Keynesian economics notwithstanding, the economic cycle scarcely deviated from its classic pattern. For those with long memories, the run-up to 1973 was all too reminiscent of the run-up to 1929. As the market became saturated with everything from aeroplanes and motor cars to hi-fi and cameras, investors switched to property (the selfsame alligator-infested swamps in Florida), 'high-flying' (but low-yielding) stocks and shares of dubious parentage (this was the era of John Bloom and Bernie Cornfeld), and any other speculation which offered a quick return; and, not surprisingly, the more speculative the venture, the higher the interest rate they were charged. In terms of market philosophy it was a natural reaction: who would want to invest in General Motors, when unsold cars were piling up and the corporation's annual gross return over the last decade, measured by capital gains (if there were any) and dividends received, was around 0.3 per cent before tax and before allowing for depreciation of the dollar? In any other terms, it was a disaster. What the boom created was not real resources but paper resources; and, since the paper was intrinsically valueless, it depreciated rapidly. That is what we mean by inflation.

In this unhappy but all-too-familiar process Keynesianism played little part, but it played some. From Keynes, after all, derived the idea that, if demand were insufficient (if people simply would not buy another Ford car or eat more of those nauseating breakfast foods), the government should intervene to stimulate demand. It could do so in a number of ways: by programmes which put more money in the hands of consumers and sent them out on a spending spree, or by manipulating the rate of interest in such a way as to induce businessmen to borrow and invest. I am not sufficient of an economist to adjudge these remedies, but it is a matter of observation that they have not operated in fact as they should in theory. The consumer, it seems, has shown a disconcerting propensity not to spend. When he received his tax rebate he puts it in the savings bank instead of dashing off to buy a new washing machine. The businessman's reactions are not dissimilar. Of course it makes some difference to his investment propensity whether the rate of interest he has to pay is 20 per cent or 5 per cent. But what dictates his investment decisions is the anticipated rate of profit; and, if he sees no increased profit from an additional factory or new machinery – if, in other words, he concludes that there are already far too many pantyhose or fresh-frozen pizzas on the market – he is not going to invest even if he can borrow money at the classical $2\frac{1}{2}$ per cent of nineteenth-century consols. Far better to use available funds to buy up a competitor on the cheap – which does nothing for employment or for the expansion of the economy.

This, in rough outline, was the route by which we reached the destination called 'stagflation'. It is fashionable today to blame full employment, and by implication Keynes, the prophet of full employment. Full employment, it is said, has cushioned the unions and made it possible for them to demand ever-higher wages, thus stoking the fires of cost-push inflation. It might be more relevant to point out the way full employment has cushioned big business. We all know that unemployment, by reducing demand, should push down prices. but what happened in 1974 when unemployment was soaring and huge unsold inventories were piling up? The response of General Motors (quickly followed by its lesser brethren) was to raise prices per vehicle by $1,000 or the equivalent.

There is certainly nothing Keynesian about this, nothing that by any stretch of the imagination can be gleaned from Keynes's writings. Indeed, it has often been pointed out that 'oligopoly', or the trend towards the concentration of economic power in the hands of huge corporations, does not enter into Keynes's calculations. That, it is argued, is one of the reasons for the 'failure' of Keynesian economics. There may be a grain of truth in this, but it is far from the whole truth. If Keynesian economics failed, it was because they were not Keynesian enough. 'The outstanding faults of the economic society in which we live', Keynes wrote in *The General Theory*, 'are its failure to provide for full employment and its arbitrary and inequitable distribution of wealth and income.' The so-called Keynesian era was the time when the first half of Keynes's lesson was avidly learnt and the second half utterly neglected. We shall never understand why it failed so critically to perform according to promise unless we take account of this selective, one-sided application of Keynes's teaching.

What happened, once economists recovered from the shocks of the 1930s, was that they turned their minds to remodelling and reassembling the Keynesian apparatus of demand management to suit the needs of the well-organised interests which employed them. Full employment, as already indicated, was acceptable to all parties for political reasons; it became, in Joan Robinson's words, 'the new defence of *laisser faire*'. It was also extremely good for business. Income redistribution had a nasty Marxist smell, but the bright boys along the Charles river shrewdly perceived that, in a growing economy, it could safely be ingored. Provided you baked a bigger cake there would be more for all, and no one was going to quibble if the lion's share went to the lucky few. At the end of the score the distribution of income in the United States and in the United Kingdom was virtually the same in 1975 as it had been in 1945; but there was certainly more to go round.

Keynes himself was partly to blame for the perversion of his ideas. He was serious about income redistribution, if only for the reason that the poor (as he saw it) spend more of their income than the rich and therefore contribute more to stimulating aggregate demand. But he never really bent his mind to the question in detail, just as, concerned to raise aggregate productivity, he never bent his mind seriously to the question of what production should be for. What he left behind were little more than asides – cryptic remarks about a 'somewhat comprehensive socialisation of investment', or the well-known quips about pyramids and cathedrals and burying old bottles filled with banknotes – which an everyday business economist could safely dismiss as visionary or impractical. He might have answered in defence that he could not be expected to analyse everything in detail, that it was surely enough for one man to have unravelled the knot of unemployment. But the consequence, so far as the vital questions of income distribution and the social purposes of economic activity were concerned, was that Keynes left the field clear for the corporate Keynesians, who couldn't have cared less about either.

The result was a gross misallocation of resources, compared with which the pyramids were a childish prank. Never before in the history of the world have the world's perishable resources been used up so quickly to so little purpose as during the past twenty-five years. *Ne pas gaspiller le pain,* the notice in the Paris métro used to read in my younger days. The age of Keynes, as it is miscalled, was the age of *gaspillage, par excellence.* The cause was the perversion of Keynes's ideas which taught that the only way to keep the economy ticking over was to consume as much as possible, preferably of things of no durable value. Today, too late, we have woken up – or have we? – to the realisation that resources are scarce and finite, that if we continue as we have been doing, even without acceleration (but without acceleration, what of growth?), we are heading for catastrophe. That is the legacy of the so-called Keynesian era, and unfortunately it is the next generation that will have to pay for the sins of its fathers. That is why my generation – the Keynesian generation, or the pseudo-Keynesians who thought they had all the answers – should put its head in the gas oven, while there is still gas to go round. It is not a record of which there is any reason to be proud, and future historians, looking back on the Keynesian era, will see it as an aberration and as a challenge and an opportunity that were missed.

Index

112